W9-DDE-599

REST IN
PEACE

A HISTORY OF AMERICAN CEMETERIES

Meg Greene

TWENTY-FIRST CENTURY BOOKS · MINNEAPOLIS

To Mark

Twenty-First Century Books
A division of Lerner Publishing Group, Inc.
241 First Avenue North
Minneapolis, MN 55401 U.S.A.

Website address: www.lernerbooks.com

Library of Congress Cataloging-in-Publication Data

Greene, Meg.
    Rest in peace : a history of American cemeteries / by
Meg Greene.
        p.   cm. — (People's history)
    Includes bibliographical references and index.
    ISBN: 978-0-8225-3414-3 (lib. bdg. : alk. paper)
  1. Cemeteries—United States—Juvenile literature.
  2. Burial—United States—Juvenile literature. 3. United
States—Social life and customs—Juvenile literature.
  I. Title.
GT3203.G74 2008
393.09—dc22   2007022093

Manufactured in the United States of America
1 2 3 4 5 6 - JR – 13 12 11 10 09 08

CHAPTER ONE

EARLY AMERICAN BURIALS (3000 B.C.–A.D. 1775)

Burial grounds and cemeteries have played an important role in human culture since its beginnings thousands of years ago. Early peoples had various methods of caring for the dead. These rituals and their sacred spaces reflected a great diversity from region to region. They changed from culture to culture. Peoples of different cultures might have different ideas about the site of a burial ground. They might use different types of grave markers and symbols. There might even be rules about what plants and trees decorate the grounds.

Burial practices might include ways of protecting the body inside some type of covering. They also would cover whether the body is buried, cremated (burning the deceased), or exposed to the elements to speed the body's decay. A person's place in society could determine how elaborate a burial would be.

Many early civilizations regarded burial grounds as necessary. They were a way to separate the living from the dead. The ancient Egyptians built a necropolis, a city of the dead, outside their cities. The necropolis might include roads and walking paths. It was enclosed by a high wall. The word *cemetery*, or "sleeping chamber," originated with the Greeks. It symbolized the idea of the dead as merely sleeping while they move from human to eternal life.

In ancient Greece many people believed that "shades," or spirits of the dead, could not cross water. To keep them from the world of the living, Greek cemeteries were built as small islands surrounded by water. The ancient Romans buried their dead in the hills near their cities to keep them from entering the world of the living.

Native American Burials

In North America, traditional Native American burial customs varied widely. The differences depended on geography and environment, social structure, and spiritual beliefs. For instance, many Plains and Pacific Northwest tribes practiced aboveground burials. The bodies were placed in trees, on scaffolds, or in boxes on stilts. The body was wrapped in either cloth or buffalo robes. Then it was laid to rest on top of the structure. Aboveground

Two Native Americans stand next to an elaborately decorated burial platform.

Indian Mounds Park in Saint Paul, Minnesota, preserves six burial mounds that date from about two thousand years ago.

burial allowed the body to decay over time and to be protected from predatory animals. These burials were reserved for men only. The bodies of women and children were often left in the underbrush or woods to be eaten by animals.

The Chickasaw and other tribes in the Southeast buried the dead in a grave directly under the house of the deceased. In the Southwest, some Navahos still leave a body in the home where the person died. They cover the body with stones and then close up the house. If the body is removed for an outside burial, the house may be burned down. This is to prevent evil spirits, traditionally associated with the dead, from interfering with the living.

Mound burial was an early Native American practice. Mound building dated from approximately 3000 B.C. to the A.D. 1500s. These mounds still exist in many places, most often in the Ohio and Mississippi River valleys.

Some of the early mounds were simple earth coverings over one or two bodies. Later, the mounds might cover an entire ceremonial building. Sometimes only a few bodies were buried in the covered building. In other mounds, the remains of many dead have been found. In some places, important leaders buried within the mound might be enclosed in log tombs. Artifacts were often buried with the bodies. These might include stone pipes with images of animals such as owls, hawks, eagles, dogs, or raccoons. Archaeologists have also found copper ear ornaments and bracelets, necklaces of freshwater pearls, bear teeth, copper axes, pottery vessels, and flint tools.

Some larger mounds had passageways that led to small chambers, or rooms. These rooms might contain dead that were sometimes first cremated. Some experts believe that these mounds were built to honor important tribal members such as shamans or chiefs.

About A.D. 700, Native Americans in the Mississippi Valley began to build effigy mounds—mounds in the shapes of animals such as birds, bears, and panthers. The effigy mounds usually contain only a few remains.

One of the best surviving examples of an effigy mound is the Serpent Mound of the Adena culture in southern Ohio. It was built in approximately A.D. 1100. The mound, measuring 1,254 feet long, 20 feet wide, and 4 to 5 feet high, is in the shape of a snake.

This aerial view of the Serpent Mound of the Adena culture shows why it received its name. It is located in Locust Grove, Ohio.

Though not common, urn burial was another method of honoring the dead. Some tribes of the Southeast and Southwest, particularly burial mound builders, used earthenware urns or jars to hold the bones of the deceased. These urns were often round in shape. They measured ten to twenty inches in diameter. The urn might be covered by animal skins or by another urn. The urns were placed in pits in the mound chambers. Archaeologists believe that the bodies were first left to decay. Then the remaining bones were gathered to be placed inside the urns. In cases where the urns held only a single skull or a small group of bones, scientists think that the clay urn was molded around the skull or bones to tightly enclose the remains.

In Alaska the Athabascan people built spirit houses over the grave of a deceased relative. The small wood structures were painted with colors or symbols that identified the family and the deceased. The houses were left to decay and become part of nature again. Spirit houses are also an interesting example of the blending of two cultures. In this case, the Athabascans adopted the idea of the spirit houses from the Christian practices of Russian Orthodox missionaries. The missionaries arrived in Alaska in the 1800s to teach and convert Native American groups to Christianity.

The Ojibwa built burial huts over the graves in their cemeteries. Openings at the ends of the huts allowed the spirits of the dead to escape to the afterworld. The photo above was taken in Minnesota.

Early Colonial Burials

The first European colonists in North America arrived in the 1500s. Their main concern was to survive. The colonists spent most of their time building shelters, hunting or growing food, and protecting themselves from danger. They had little time to organize formal cemeteries. Most of the time, their dead were buried quickly and without much ceremony. The graves were often unmarked and usually near the spot where the person died. Few settlers had the carving skills to make fancy grave markers. Often they just didn't have time.

Often early colonists had no wish to call attention to their dead. Native Americans resented the white settlers and their desire for Indian lands. Disputes over land often led to violence between Europeans and Native Americans. Colonists preferred isolated and unmarked grave sites to make it difficult for Native Americans to know how many settlers had been killed. Unmarked graves were less likely to be disturbed, and they required no care or protection.

Still, for some colonists, it was important to note the death of a community member. Early Spanish colonists left flowers and crosses at the sites of violent deaths, such as murders or attacks. This was similar to the roadside markers that, in modern times, mark the site of a traffic fatality. If individual grave markers existed at all, they were crudely made of stone or wood and contained only the initials of the deceased.

The Graves of New Spain

By the 1600s and early 1700s, Spanish settlements in North and South America had become more established. People had time to devote to the care and memory of the dead. Colonial Spanish cemeteries became more elaborate. They began to look as much as possible like those in Spain. The Spanish settlers were Catholics. The cemeteries were sacred ground blessed by a priest. Unlike the earlier wilderness graves, the Spanish enclosed their cemeteries with either a wood fence or stone wall. The fence kept out trespassers, livestock, and wild animals. The dead bodies, wrapped

This colonial Spanish graveyard in Taos Pueblo, New Mexico, shows the typical wall that surrounds the graves marked by crosses. The church at the center was built in 1619 and destroyed in 1847.

in fabric shrouds, were buried with their arms crossed over their chests. Burials were placed in orderly rows in the cemetery.

Colonial Spanish cemeteries followed ancient Christian burial traditions. For example, gravestones faced east toward the rising sun to be ready for the coming Judgment Day. On this day, Christians believe that God will decide the fates of all people based on how good they were in life. Headstones fashioned from both stone and wood marked individual graves. Common designs on gravestones included crosses that stood for the sacrifice, suffering, death, and resurrection of Christ. Doves were symbols of peace and the Holy Spirit. Symbols also depicted sheep as the lambs of God, angels, trees of life, and the human heart. The Spanish often placed a large cross, six to ten feet high, in the middle of the cemetery.

In all its symbols, Spanish Catholicism emphasized the love of Christ, the resurrection of all souls, and eternal life.

The Graves of New England

The Puritans of colonial New England didn't believe in ornamentation in their graveyards. The Puritans were a religious group that fled persecution in England in the 1600s. For them, burying grounds were simply places to deposit the remains of the dead. The Puritans believed that the body was a shell, temporary and unimportant. The immortal soul alone mattered. The Puritans used their cemeteries to remind people of the shortness of life in this world and the constant presence of death. They reminded the living of the need to prepare the soul for life in the hereafter.

In early New England, Puritans also rejected churchyard burials and ornamentation. They felt that these encouraged worship of ancestors and of stone images. Instead, many Puritan New England towns of the 1600s set aside land for a community burial ground. These early Puritan graveyards had no order. Graves were dug randomly. Ornamental plantings were rare. Most graves were topped with a small, simple wooden marker. The ground was mostly bare except for the weeds that grew up on their own. This was deliberate. To the Puritans, the graveyard symbolized the wilderness, which was the source of chaos, darkness, and death.

By the middle of the 1600s, a growing Puritan emphasis on death led to more elaborate cemetery art. The Puritans began to create carved gravestones known as death's head markers. These gravestones emphasized the fearful presence of death and the possibility of eternal damnation. For example, Joseph Tapping's gravestone in King's Chapel Burying Ground (the oldest burial ground in Boston, Massachusetts) carries a winged death's head.

Another example of Puritan gravestone imagery is the portal-shaped stone. The headstone might have small openings near the top symbolizing a door, or portal. The portal stone is a symbol of an entrance to a new life or passage to the unknown. It stood for the opening through which the

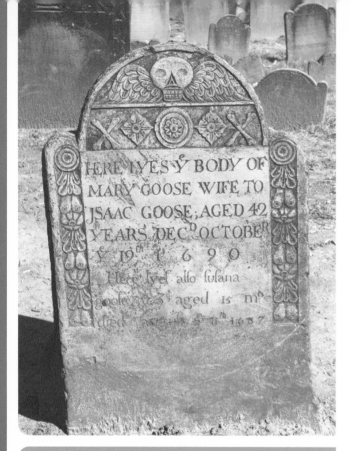

This headstone at the grave of Mary Goose, thought to be the author of Mother Goose rhymes, shows the winged death's head typical of many Puritan headstones. It is found at the Granary Burying Ground in Boston.

dead pass from the earth to the afterlife. Sometimes the stone might have decorative columns. More elaborate portal stones might show one side beckoning the departed to heaven. The other side would have images of the wilderness and demons sending the soul to hell.

The Graves of the American South

Many of the British colonists who settled in the American South during the 1800s were members of the Church of England, the Anglican Church. Anglican burial grounds didn't emphasize the horrors of death and the pains of hell. They honored the dead, the hoped-for resurrection (rising from the dead), and life everlasting. In many isolated towns and villages, members of families and the larger British community joined to create town burial grounds. In some cases, these burial grounds might belong to a church. In others, a community burial ground might be open to any white member of the community.

Another common type of burial ground in the American South was the family burial plot. The family cemetery was unique to North America. Europeans, except for nobility and royalty, did not have family burial grounds. In Europe, bodies were buried in common graveyards. Family plots came about in the American colonies out of need. For families living on isolated farms or plantations, it wasn't practical to haul a dead body through miles of wilderness to the nearest town.

Whenever possible, family burial plots in the South were placed on the edge of the fields at the highest point on the property. Usually a fence—simple wooden pickets or stone—enclosed the site. Trees were planted for shade. Other ornamental plantings, such as mimosa trees, gardenias, cedars, or crape myrtles, added beauty and color to the grounds. The overall effect was that of a lovely garden planted in the midst of the wilderness. In early southern graveyards, small wooden markers marked the graves. Later, headstones carved from sandstone or granite became more popular. Wealthy planters' headstones were often elaborate affairs with intricate carvings and engraving.

Unlike the Puritans, who left their burial grounds to the mercy of nature, family burial grounds in the southern colonies were often carefully tended and maintained. To keep the grounds clear, the family scraped the graveyard soil once or twice a year to remove weeds.

In the South, where slavery was practiced, white masters expected their black slaves to arrange and organize the burials of their owner's family. Slaves took care of many parts of the funeral and burial services, from cleaning and preparing the bodies to digging the graves. They also tended to the land in the white cemeteries.

In the 1930s, the southern writer Eudora Welty (1909–2001) took this photograph of an old family burial ground in Mississippi.

The cemetery at Monticello, President Thomas Jefferson's estate, contains headstones of family members, including his daughter Martha Jefferson Randolph and her family.

On many large plantations, such as Thomas Jefferson's Monticello or George Washington's Mount Vernon, both in Virginia, family burial grounds continued to be cared for long after the original families had died. Most family plots did not fare so well. As better economic opportunities beckoned, families moved on. They abandoned their farms and plantations along with the family burial grounds. Sometimes the only reminder of a family cemetery was a decaying stone wall, a blooming mimosa or cedar tree in an odd location, or an overgrown headstone. Though abandoned, these burial grounds were still respected by locals. Southern hunters trod carefully on land where farms once stood. If they encountered a headstone, local superstition required that they jump over it backward to prevent the death of a member of their own family.

Slave Cemeteries

On southern plantations with African slaves, the white master often gave a small piece of ground on the property to the slaves to bury their dead. This land was sometimes called "God's Little Acre." All the plantation slaves were buried there. Sometimes, however, trusted or lifelong house servants were buried near their master's family.

Many of the customs and traditions that were practiced at slave funerals are lost to historians. Slave owners did not normally keep records of the births or deaths of their slaves. Most slaves were not able to read or write, so they couldn't keep track themselves. Still, some things are known about certain common funeral rituals. Some slave funerals began with a coffin, handmade by friends and family. The body rested nearby until the coffin was ready for it. The coffin builders protected the body from animal predators. Because the slaves were forced to work all day, many slave funerals took place at night. The deceased was sometimes buried with his or her head or eyes facing east, in the direction of Africa. Graves were often unmarked.

Sometimes small markers made from stone or wood identified and paid tribute to the deceased. These graves were decorated with the person's plates, eating utensils, cups, mirrors, and bottles to accompany them on their journey into the afterlife.

Other rituals practiced at slave grave sites might include killing a white chicken, which symbolized the spirit world, to protect the grave. Planting evergreens on graves assured the dead a peaceful rest. Some slave grave sites had bottle trees. Families hung empty bottles from tree branches to keep away evil spirits. On Sundays, family and friends would visit the cemetery to tidy up the grounds.

Slave funerals were often joyous occasions. In the view of many slaves, death was something to be celebrated as well as mourned. It was a release from the suffering and oppression under which slaves lived. Some of the mourners felt that their dead loved ones had finally achieved freedom from the bonds of slavery that had made their lives so painful. Believing that their loved ones were much happier in death, some slaves would sing, chant, and rejoice at funerals.

Slaves and free blacks in the urban North also had burial grounds separate from white cemeteries. Graveyards for blacks were often

located in undesirable sites outside the city. One of the oldest surviving urban slave burial grounds is the Common Burial Ground located in Newport, Rhode Island, and established in 1712. In New York City, slaves and free blacks were buried in the Negros Burial Ground. It was first located beyond the city wall near a swamp. Later, it was moved several times, leaving behind the graves of the dead. These unclaimed remains fell to the plow or were built over as the city expanded. David Valentine wrote a history of Broadway in the 1850s. In it he described the long-abandoned burial ground for blacks in New York. "Beyond the Commons lay what in the earliest settlement of the town had been appropriated as a burial place for Negroes, slaves and free. It was a desolate . . . spot."

A City of Souls

Some American communities have had special problems to think about when planning burial grounds. Probably the most famous of these is New Orleans, Louisiana, which is situated on the Mississippi River and lies below water level.

From the time of the founding of the city in 1718, residents have struggled with different methods for burying their dead. Digging a regular six-foot grave was almost impossible, because river water soon filled the site. Even if a coffin was buried deeper, heavy rains or flooding pushed it out of the ground and the coffin floated away.

Because of the high water table in New Orleans, Louisiana, the city started burying its dead aboveground in crypts in the 1700s. The graveyards are often referred to as cities of the dead.

One early solution was weighing down the coffins with heavy stones. But even weighted coffins would pop out of the grave after a hard rain. Another method was boring holes in a coffin and then weighing it down with stones and sand. This didn't work either. City officials decided that the city's dead would be safe and protected in aboveground vaults, similar to the ones found in both Spanish and French cemeteries in Europe. In 1789 Saint Louis Cemetery #1 was created as New Orleans's first aboveground cemetery.

This coffin is in the old Saint Louis Cemetery, in New Orleans, Louisiana. To save space, many coffins will be put in the same vault as members of the family die.

The cemeteries of New Orleans are often called cities of the dead with good reason. Inside the heavy wrought iron gates of the cemeteries stand vaults in all shapes and sizes. Many vaults are topped with crosses or statues. The cemeteries are organized by streets (and street signs) just like the cities of the living.

To save space in New Orleans's cemeteries, it is common practice to bury all the members of a family in the same tomb or vault. The names and dates of the deceased are inscribed on a plaque or headstone. Many of the smaller vaults could only hold one or two bodies at a time. To make room for more bodies, it was customary, after a year and a day, to unseal the vault. Any human remains in the casket, usually bones, were removed and placed either at the back of the vault or below it. The coffin was destroyed to make way for the next burial. In modern times, the human remains are placed in a specially made burial bag. This is put to the side or back of the vault. The coffin is destroyed, and the vault is ready for newly deceased family members.

New Orleans has more than forty aboveground cemeteries. Unlike other U.S. cities and towns, where the dead are hidden and out of sight, the aboveground cemeteries of New Orleans provide a constant reminder of how close the living and the dead truly are.

CHAPTER TWO

THE BURYING GROUND (1775–1830)

By the middle of the 1700s, many of the small colonial villages and settlements had grown into larger cities and towns. The Puritan influence had weakened. Many residents relied on church burial grounds rather than community graveyards. City officials began to realize that while the number of dead would continue to rise, the ground in which to bury them would not increase.

Too Little Ground

Large numbers of colonists had died in the American Revolution (1775–1783), which established the independent United States. They also died in large numbers from deadly diseases such as yellow fever and smallpox. As a result, many church cemeteries were full. In some cemeteries, coffins were buried one atop another. Often they were within a few inches of the ground's surface. Sometimes so many coffins were heaped on top of one another that the graves became burial mounds, rising several feet above the ground. Among the worst cases of overcrowding was the graveyard at Trinity Church in New York City. By 1800 the Trinity graveyard held the remains of about one hundred thousand people.

In some towns and cities, land was in short supply because of growing populations. Graveyards near churches or in the town square often became the place for public gatherings. When prime grazing land was limited, local farmers rented cemetery land where their livestock would graze among the graves.

The cemetery of Trinity Church in New York, New York, became overcrowded in the early 1800s.

In Death as in Life

Graveyards have always reflected the religious and cultural beliefs of the living. Each religious group had its own graveyard. In the United States of the early 1800s, members of different ethnic groups also tended to bury their dead in their own graveyards, which allowed them to observe their own rituals and ceremonies.

Class distinctions carried over into death. For example, society's cast-offs, including paupers (the poor and homeless), orphans, illegitimate children, and strangers ended up in unmarked graves in potter's fields. The term *potter's field* is believed to have its origins in the Gospel of Saint Matthew in the Bible. Judas Iscariot, one of the apostles (followers) of Jesus, overcome by remorse, returned thirty pieces of silver paid to him to betray Jesus. The priests used the coins to buy a field as a burial place for strangers. The field was called a potter's field because pot makers dug for clay there and the clay-rich soil was unfit for growing crops. In the United States, potter's fields were located on the outskirts of a city or in a small, segregated area of a cemetery.

Rules determined who could be buried in a potter's field. For instance, suicides and criminals were never buried there. Their actions in life went against religious beliefs. Instead, civil and church authorities reserved lonely spots outside of town for burying criminals. The remains of a suicide were buried in an isolated and often unmarked

This potter's field in Salisbury, Maryland, is the only cemetery owned by the city. Potter's fields are used to bury those who could not afford to buy burial space.

grave. In some cases, a suicide's body was buried at a crossroads with a small marker, such as a crudely made wood cross or sign, noting the site as the grave of a suicide. These burials almost always took place at night. Crossroads were chosen because it was believed that if the dead arose, they would not know which way to go. Sometimes to make extra sure that the dead did not awaken, wood stakes were driven through the body.

The New Burying Ground Society

In the early days of the new nation, U.S. cemeteries had become little more than refuse piles for the dead. Looking over a church graveyard in the late eighteenth century, a foreign visitor to the United States was appalled at what he saw. He later described the site as a "soppy church-yard, where the mourners sink ankle deep in a rank and offensive mould, mixed with broken bones and fragments of coffins."

The original burial ground in New Haven, Connecticut, was in the town's center. It was close to the town's first meetinghouse, which had served the community since 1639. For more than 150 years, the grounds beside and behind the meetinghouse held the remains of New Haven residents. By the 1790s, estimates suggest that New Haven had between four thousand and five thousand graves within seven thousand square feet of space. Visitors and residents alike were critical of the burial ground. One visiting minister wrote in 1795, "The beauty of the [town] green is greatly impaired by the Burial ground in the centre, which, it is contem-plated, to hide from public view by weeping willows." Another visitor described the old burial ground as having been "degraded into a mere common object, and speedily loses all its connection with the invisible world in a gross and vulgar union with the ordinary business of life."

James Hillhouse, a local politician and businessman, suggested setting aside land for a new burying ground. Hillhouse believed that a new burial ground that beautified New Haven would attract well-to-do residents and enterprising businessmen. These people would help the city prosper. In 1796 he convinced thirty-one other members of prominent New Haven

James Hillhouse encouraged the creation of a burial society in New Haven, Connnecticut.

families to form a private association. The aim of this group, the New Burying Ground Society, was to establish and maintain a burial ground for the city.

Under Hillhouse's direction, the society formed a corporation to purchase land to be set aside for the creation of a cemetery. Incorporation meant that the New Burying Ground Society made its own decisions and owned and controlled the property. The individuals or families who purchased lots were members of the corporation. No longer could a minister or government official determine who would be buried where or whose remains would be removed. The burial grounds were legally protected sacred ground, even though the site was nowhere near a church.

Josiah Meig, another prominent resident of New Haven, was called upon to design the cemetery. Meig's plan was to enclose and level a ten-acre field. He then divided the area into sections. Each section was fenced. The sections were separated by paths wide enough for a carriage to pass through. Anyone who could afford a plot could purchase one. Several of the plots were reserved for specific groups, such as religious congregations and the graduates of nearby Yale College. But even those with few means, including African Americans, were permitted to buy plots in different sections of the cemetery.

By placing the burial ground outside of town, the graveyard was separated from the ordinary business of daily life. Hillhouse and his committee had created an island of order, serenity, peace, and respect for the dead. Unkempt, half-forgotten plots of land containing too many bodies crammed together became a thing of the past.

The creation of the New Burying Ground ushered in a new era of graveyard landscape decoration. Tall Lombardy poplars lined the roads. Weeping willows (known as funeral trees), were planted throughout. Through these plantings, the burial ground offered an image of nature improved upon by the hand of man. Large monuments, carved from expensive stone or marble and elaborately adorned with the family name, became attractions themselves. People came to New Haven especially to visit the cemetery, as they would travel to other places of interest.

This Egyptian-inspired gate at the entrance to the New Burying Ground in New Haven, Connecticut, was built in 1845, many years after the cemetery opened in the 1790s.

Success and Failure

Not everyone approved of a cemetery that was not affiliated with a church and a religion. Some disliked the burial ground's precise lines and geometric layout. Even so, representatives from other cities went to New Haven to study the burial ground. They hoped to copy its plan in their cities. Some of these other plans failed. In some cases, members of the middle and upper classes refused to buy plots near where the poor were buried. In others the costs of maintaining the grounds were too high or the location turned out to be a poor one. Still, the success of New Haven provided new directions and new ideas for burial grounds throughout the nation.

'Tis holy ground—this city of the Dead
Let no rude accents of untimely mirth
Break the calm stillness of this sacred earth.

—FROM "SWEET AUBURN AND MOUNT AUBURN,"
BY CAROLINE ORNE, 1844

CHAPTER THREE

THE RURAL CEMETERY MOVEMENT (1830–1855)

In the mid-1800s, Americans found themselves in an era of explosive industrial growth. Factories and spinning and weaving mills, using technology from Great Britain, sprang up in cities and towns throughout the Northeast. People left their farms and flocked to the cities to take the new jobs available in factories and mills. The populations of the cities expanded rapidly. Workers lived crowded into dark tenements (rental buildings with many apartments) and spent ten to fourteen hours a day at work. Americans grew nostalgic for the serenity of the countryside they had left behind. Many people feared that the bustle of urban life and its lack of access to fresh air and exercise would strain the nerves and weaken body and soul.

As the cities grew, they had less land for burial grounds. The established city grave sites became as overcrowded as the city itself. In 1831 a New England writer observed: "[T]he burying place continues to be the most neglected spot in all the region, distinguished from other fields only by its leaning stones and the meanness of its enclosures, without a tree or a shrub to take from it the air of utter desolation."

Mount Auburn

By 1825 the residents of Boston confronted an acute crisis. The population of the city had increased to such an extent that the city's water and air had become polluted from human and factory waste. Foul smells floated up from decaying bodies in the city's dilapidated graveyard crypts.

The Old Granary Burial Grounds in Boston. In the 1800s, graveyards were a target for grave robbers and vandals looking for valuables.

The semiexposed graves were offensive and unhealthy. At that time, little was done to preserve bodies after death. The practice of embalming, where blood and body fluids are drained from the body and replaced with a chemical preservative to slow decomposition, was not common until after the Civil War (1861–1865). Graves were the targets for vandals and thieves. They dug up and looted coffins for jewelry and other valuables buried with the dead. Then they often left the decaying corpses lying about. Concerns about the decomposition and stench of corpses in the heart of Boston led city officials to look for better ways to bury the dead. But nothing came of their efforts.

A citizens' group hoped to succeed where the city officials had failed. The group was led by Jacob Bigelow. He was a local doctor, gardener, and friend to many of the city's wealthy residents. Bigelow gathered one hundred residents to discuss plans for a new burial ground outside the city. The search for a suitable site took more than six years. Finally, in 1831, the group purchased seventy-two acres of farmland known as Sweet Auburn. It was in the countryside along the Charles River about four miles from Boston. Bigelow's proposal included a permanent staff to preserve the country setting of the graveyard.

"Garden of Graves"

Acquiring the land was only the beginning. Bigelow and his committee needed to convince people to buy plots in the new cemetery. At that time, most people were not used to the idea of burying their loved ones far from their homes. To make the land attractive to buyers, Bigelow and his supporters joined with the Massachusetts Horticultural Society—a large gardening club. Their plan was to create a scenic landscape at Sweet Auburn. Bigelow's proposal was in keeping with the passionate interest of people of that time in gardening and horticulture. For many Americans, planting trees, bushes, and flowers reflected the moral virtues and peace of the rural past. Gardeners and landscape designers were eager to display their skill at the new cemetery at Mount Auburn.

Mount Auburn, with its gardens, landscapes, and fountains (above), became a place of relaxation for the living.

Mount Auburn was a fine example of what nature, combined with labor and imagination, could accomplish. Bigelow and the committee created a burial place with a network of ponds and wetlands and a forest of pines, oaks, and beeches. A system of roads wound through the cemetery. Bigelow's group created a beautiful garden to protect the dead in their rest.

In 1831 Lydia Maria Child, a noted American writer and women's rights activist, had written in *The Mother's Book*: "So important do I consider cheerful associations with death, that I wish to see our grave-yards laid out with walks and trees, and beautiful shrubs, as places of public promenade. We ought not to draw such a line of separation between those who are living in this world, and those who are alive in another."

Mount Auburn translated her thoughts into reality. It also signaled another shift in the attitude toward cemeteries: a new emphasis on the family. For sixty dollars, families could purchase lots measuring three hundred square feet—more than enough for several generations of one family's dead. Families could become members of the Mount Auburn Corporation with the right to vote on cemetery issues. Plot owners were allowed to erect any sort of monument that would honor their dead. They might choose majestic angels carved in marble or spacious stone mausoleums (aboveground tombs) that stood like small mansions on the grounds. Those who could afford it could hire private gardeners to tend to their plots.

For those who could not afford to purchase entire lots, Mount Auburn offered single graves in the middle of the cemetery. Owners of single graves had no say in running the corporation.

Mount Auburn Cemetery opened with the burial of a young Boston woman in 1832. Soon afterward, people were flocking there to enjoy the cemetery's hills, dells, creeks, and paths. Tourists from throughout the United States—and even around the world—added Mount Auburn to their itinerary. A visit to the cemetery was considered a necessary part of a visit to Boston. Guide-

Lydia Maria Child wrote about her ideas for a cemetery that had cheerful associations with death.

books provided maps, suggested routes, gave descriptions of individual monuments, and provided thoughtful readings. Within fifteen years, the Fitchburg Railroad established a station at Mount Auburn. By mid-century, the streetcar stopped at the front gate.

A Magical Place

Early descriptions of Mount Auburn stressed its natural beauty. The "natural" setting of Mount Auburn was not the untamed, chaotic nature of the wilderness, however. It was one of order and peace. The landscape was intended to offer a sense of calm serenity. In it, people could escape the city's dirt and noise and take in nature's gentle beauty.

Visitors flocked to Mount Auburn to see the landscapes, gardens, and magnificent statues.

Observers both famous and obscure recorded their impressions after visiting Mount Auburn. The British actress Fannie Kemble, who visited the cemetery in 1833, called Mount Auburn "a pleasure garden instead of a place of graves." The British writer Harriet Martineau also visited Mount Auburn. In *Retrospect of Western Travel,* published in 1838, she stated: "I believe it is allowed that Mount Auburn is the most beautiful cemetery in the world."

In a letter to a friend dated September 8, 1846, when she was just sixteen, future poet Emily Dickinson set down her impressions of a visit: "Have you ever been to Mount Auburn? It seems as if Nature had formed the spot with a distinct idea in view of its being a resting place for her children, where wearied & disappointed they might stretch themselves beneath the spreading cypress & close their eyes calmly as to a nights repose or flowers at set of sun."

A New Direction

Many visitors were so impressed by the beauty of the cemetery that they returned home with the dream of creating similar places. By the mid-1800s, ten major U.S. cemeteries were patterned after it. These included Laurel Hill in Philadelphia, Pennsylvania (1836); Green-Wood in Brooklyn, New York (1839); Albany Rural in Albany, New York (1841); Allegheny in Pittsburgh, Pennsylvania (1844); and Spring Grove in Cincinnati, Ohio (1844). By 1849 the Auburn model had reached westward to the Mississippi River with the creation of the Bellefontaine Cemetery in Saint Louis, Missouri. By 1863 it reached the West Coast, with Mountain View in Oakland, California. Clearly, the rural cemetery concept spoke to the American public.

Urban dwellers came to view rural cemeteries as public gardens. These cemeteries were the first large open public spaces in the United States. They served as models for the nation's city park systems. By the mid-1800s, the rural cemetery had replaced the urban graveyard in the United States. In these rural cemeteries, designers emphasized nature through grand entry gates, winding paths, lakes, gentle hills, trees, and

Laurel Hill Cemetery in Philadelphia, Pennsylvania, was the first cemetery to be patterned after Mount Auburn. It featured the same spectacular mausoleums and relaxing walking paths.

many original monuments. Americans were able to beautify the rituals of death through the graceful architecture, design, and symbolism of the rural cemetery. The lovely landscape helped heal the pain of death, as the living visited to pay their respects to the deceased.

Life-size angels decorate this tomb in Green-Wood Cemetery in Brooklyn, New York.

The rural cemetery movement mirrored Americans' changing attitudes toward death. People were moving away from the gloomy pessimism of the early Puritans toward optimism about life in this world and the next. Images of hope and immortality were important in the rural cemeteries. Where images of death's harsh lessons once decorated tombstones, angels and cherubs now kept company. The statuary included life-sized angels, pets, and other figures. These competed with botanical motifs such as ivy for memory, oak leaves for immortality, poppies for sleep, and acorns for life. In fact, before public art museums were founded in the 1870s, visitors went to Mount Auburn to view the art of the sculptor and monument carver. For relatives and other visitors, the statuary art in the rural cemeteries provided a cultural experience as well as a spiritual uplifting. "Cemeteries here are all the 'rage'" wrote a young British visitor, "people lounge in them and use them (as their tastes are inclined) for walking, making love, weeping, sentimentalizing, and every thing in short."

Peace Disrupted

Vandals targeted many rural cemeteries just months after they opened. These people had no qualms about carving their names or initials into the trees, breaking down fences, trampling lots, stealing flowers from grave sites, or smashing headstones. Dogs ran about freely. Visitors on horseback rode on paths designed for pedestrians. Then they tethered their horses next to trees and bushes. The horses often damaged the plantings. The echo of gunfire became commonplace as hunters moved through the grounds looking for rabbits, squirrels, and birds. Marksmen used headstones for target practice. Rural cemeteries ended up with many of the same problems—such as overcrowding and a cluttered look—that had beset earlier American burial grounds.

Some grounds also became loitering or sleeping places for the unemployed, criminals, or the homeless. Ordinary citizens and members of the cemetery corporations worried about their personal safety when visiting. The order and peace inspired by the cemetery seemed to be in peril.

New Rules

Members of the cemetery corporations throughout the United States wanted to protect their cemeteries from further damage. So starting in the 1850s, they campaigned to have even more legal control over their properties. Slowly, local and state courts

Cemetery vandalism continues to be a problem. In 2006 vandals destroyed thirteen headstones at this 1885 cemetery in Minnesota.

This gazebo drew many visitors to Mount Auburn. It provided a shady place to rest during walks through the cemetery.

granted them permission to draw up and enforce their own laws in cooperation with the local police. People who broke cemetery rules were fined from five to fifty dollars, depending on the offense. A reward of twenty dollars was offered for information about anyone who broke cemetery rules or damaged the property.

Owners of cemeteries began to enforce stricter control over visitation. Some cemeteries sold entry tickets. Guards posted at the entrance gates took the tickets and stopped anyone trying to get onto the grounds without one. Cemeteries often adopted this practice to discourage entry to the poor and immigrants, workers, or anyone who seemed disreputable. To control the growing numbers of people arriving by horseback or horse-drawn carriages and buses, Mount Auburn banned horses altogether.

New Tools

As cemetery corporations imposed new restrictions, they also added new features to attract desirable visitors. The proprietors of Mount Auburn, for example, installed a fancy gazebo (a roofed structure with open sides) that included a pump house. Here people could sit in the shade while drinking cool water pumped from the well. In 1861 toilets for women and children were built near the entrance. In 1869 a reception house provided safe quarters for those waiting for public transportation. Visitors could also buy refreshments there.

Other cemeteries followed suit. One cemetery built a series of pavilions that gave visitors a place to escape the sun or rain, to relax, or to enjoy a picnic. Some cemeteries provided guests with refreshments. Others, such as Spring Grove in Cincinnati, built magnificent roads lined with trees for carriage traffic. People could also stand along these roads to watch the elaborate funeral processions of the rich and famous. The roads at Spring Grove soon became the site for impromptu horse races. This led to the establishment of a speed limit. No horse traveling through Spring Grove cemetery was allowed to go faster than six miles per hour.

The popularity of the rural cemeteries convinced owners and trustees that money was to be made from

This photo map of Spring Grove Cemetery from the 1860s helped visitors find the funeral processions on the beautiful wide roads.

them. Along with gazebos, pavilions, pump houses, and refreshment stands, cemetery owners also began offering photographic images for those unable to visit the rural cemeteries or for those who wanted a souvenir of their visit. There seemed to be no limit to the profits and popularity of these "dormitories of the dead."

The rural cemetery movement also brought a new word into the American language: *cemetery*, from the Greek for "sleeping chamber." The rural cemetery promoters wanted the public to think of death as a long, restful sleep, a temporary slumber on the journey to eternal life.

Frederick Law Olmsted, designer of New York's Central Park, borrowed some of his ideas from rural cemeteries. This portrait of him was painted by John Singer Sargent in 1895.

The Decline of the Rural Cemetery

By the eve of the Civil War in 1861, however, maintaining "natural" spaces as part of the landscape design had become too time-consuming and too costly. Large numbers of workers were required to keep the cemeteries neat and clean. Security also cost money. And since lot owners in rural cemeteries had the right to do as they wished with their plots, the designs lacked uniformity. Upkeep of them was uneven too. As a result, the earlier ordered, scenic representation of nature took on a cluttered, unkempt look.

Perhaps most challenging to the rural cemetery movement, though, was

In addition to Central Park in New York City, Olmsted also designed Central Park in Louisville, Kentucky. This picture of the park in Louisville shows citizens enjoying its beauty in the early 1900s.

the growth of public parks in many large cities. Many landscape designers, such as Frederick Law Olmsted, who in 1857 designed Central Park in New York City, borrowed ideas from rural cemeteries. Their new parks created urban green spaces where death was nowhere to be found. As more public parks opened, fewer people chose to go to cemeteries for leisure, rest, and relaxation. Cemeteries adapted to the changing tastes of the public.

> My Lord hath called and I obeyed
> To meet and with Him dwell
> The last great debt I now have paid
> And bid the world farewell
>
> —NINETEENTH-CENTURY EPITAPH

CHAPTER FOUR

THE LANDSCAPED LAWN (1855–1917)

Taking a cue from the new city parks, cemeteries became more uniform in their landscaping and design. Headstone size was limited and standardized. Shrubbery cut back. The cemetery landscape was made to resemble a green lawn or park. With more professional supervision of cemeteries, families had less control over the care and look of their own plots. Cemeteries came to reflect a new civic pride, especially among members of the American middle class. They liked knowing that their cemeteries were well-organized communities that were monitored and serviced by trained experts.

The First Experiment

In 1855 the board of directors at Cincinnati's Spring Grove Cemetery decided to redesign the grounds. They turned to a German-born, British-trained horticulturist named Adolphe Strauch. Strauch had been a gardener and landscape architect for several large private estates in the city. He was known for open designs using light, lawn, and space. Emphasizing simplicity, his designs for these estates relied on careful and selective placement of trees, flowers, and statuary. Board members familiar with Strauch's work asked him to survey Spring Grove and suggest a plan for the new design.

Strauch's initial response was that "it was a pity [that] the beautiful reposing place of the dead was not . . . developed on a scientific plan." In his report to the board, he found the grounds too cluttered with plantings, monuments, statues, and fences. They hid the natural beauty of the site. Too many of the streets and paths were marred by overplanting, in an attempt to maintain the cemetery's "natural" scenery. Strauch criticized the lack of care given to individual plots. Many were cluttered with objects that included "numerous tin cans, old broken vases, broken pitchers, cracked glasses, lidless coffee pots, lard buckets, iron gates, fences and benches."

Strauch assured the board that all was not lost. He thought that he could eliminate most of the problems at Spring Grove. He would reduce the ornamentation of individual plots, restrict enclosed plot spaces, and restore the natural contours of the land. The board liked his ideas and hired him. Strauch not only cleaned up Spring Grove, he also offered a new cemetery design, the lawn park, to replace the rural cemetery concept.

A Bold Vision

As Strauch envisioned it, the lawn park cemetery combined landscape design and science. He used many of the same design principles at Spring Grove that he had used on private grounds. In the cemetery, he cleared away the plantings that had originally been intended to imitate nature. He replaced them with carefully designed gardens. He cut back on trees, shrubs, and other plantings to allow the artistic play of light and shadow over green lawn. Strauch also changed the natural contour of the land. He

Adolphe Strauch created a lake with swans in Spring Grove Cemetery, which he turned into a lawn park worthy of a postcard *(above)*. This postcard is from the early 1900s.

gradually raised the ground toward the back of the cemetery, much as rows of seats rise toward the back of a theater. The design allowed the burial plots in the back to be seen more easily. Finally, he added a lake complete with swans and an island. The overall effect was a planned landscape that "unified land and water, monument and nature, flora and fauna."

Strauch also proposed less ornate monuments. These individually created monuments had been a hallmark of the rural cemetery. He could not remove existing headstones, but he urged that lot owners do away with tall monuments. He suggested that they use smaller grave markers standing no more than six inches high. The small markers made cemetery plots more affordable. When Mount Auburn, the United States' first rural cemetery, opened for public burials, a single lot of three hundred square feet cost $60. By 1855 the price of a lot had increased to $150. By 1883 lot prices ranged from $225 for an "unexceptional lot" to $750 for "choice lots." By contrast, lot prices at Spring Grove ranged from $90 to $150. As one promoter of the lawn cemetery proudly announced, "It is a curious illustration of the power of habit over right reason, to see wealthy proprietors [plot owners] sinking a heavy granite coping [the top of a wall] around a lot, expending perhaps $2,500 or $3,000 for the sake of making the place look like a magnified city 'area,' and when placing a monument within it at a cost of say $2,000 more." A growing number of Americans were realizing "how incomparably superior . . . is the landscape lawn plan."

In addition, the smaller markers opened up the landscape and gave the grounds a unified look. Larger monuments were permitted in some sections of the cemetery as long as they were set back from the road. Strauch's plans limited the rights of plot owners to do as they wished. Families could not fence their lots, hire their own gardeners, or add their own plantings. Trained cemetery workers were hired to care for all the grounds and to maintain the landscape.

The board's reaction to Strauch's design for Spring Grove was overwhelmingly positive. His improvements, stated one supporter, allowed people to gradually move away from "all things that suggest death, sorrow, or pain." Still another advocate of the standardized design believed that "civilization . . . consists in subordinating the will of the individual to the comfort and well-being of all."

Lot owners were less enthusiastic. Unhappy with the new regulations, they confronted Strauch on several occasions, accusing him of "anti-American eccentricities," and "heathen principles." Others found his "scientific design" too remote and unfeeling. They were angry at the new rules Strauch had imposed on them. Originality, sometimes eccentric or sentimental, had distinguished the rural cemeteries. The lawn park, with its emphasis on standardization, banished individuality.

The Business of Death

Despite such criticisms, in 1859 the board at Spring Grove appointed Strauch superintendent of the cemetery. Strauch was responsible not only for its landscape and design, but he also supervised all employees and oversaw cemetery maintenance and upkeep. The sale of lots and the financial management of the cemetery were overseen by the board. Another superintendent managed business operations. In effect, Strauch had created the first modern cemetery, a business run by experts to make a profit from managing death.

The profits were used to hire and train additional maintenance workers and to invest in new equipment. One piece of equipment was a mechanical lawn mower. It could do the work of more than half a dozen men with handheld scythes (a cutting tool with a long curved

The lawn mower, invented in 1830, was used at Spring Grove after Adolphe Strauch became manager of the cemetery.

blade). The introduction of new varieties of grass, new mowing techniques, and new lawn care products made it easier and less expensive to maintain the grounds. The overall appearance of the lawn park was crucial to selling lots. The superintendent's job was to make sure that his cemetery looked beautiful. Then it could serve as an advertisement for itself.

As the century progressed, the cemetery business became more professional. In 1887 a group of superintendents from several major cemeteries created the Association of American Cemetery Superintendents (AACS). The AACS created guidelines on cemetery management. Books and professional journals were published for the cemetery industry. One of these publications was *Modern Cemeteries: An Essay on the Improvement and Proper Management of Rural Cemeteries*. It was published in 1888 in Hartford, Connecticut, by landscape architect and cemetery engineer Jacob Weidenmann. Weidenmann once stated that "my destiny is to work for the grave diggers." In his study, he diagrammed a variety of plot arrangements. He showed how landscaping specific areas could improve the look of untended nearby plots.

A few years later, in 1890, the AACS offered suggestions about the best size for headstones. It presented the standard height of grave mounds (not to exceed four inches) and the number of monuments allowed per family plot (one). It also advised on the best material (cut stone, concrete, and bronze) to use for monuments or vaults. The AACS also suggested limits on the number of vaults—the concrete or metal container in the ground that holds the coffin—in a cemetery. According to the AACS guidelines, lot owners could still do plantings but only if they followed the cemetery's established regulations.

A New Modern Cemetery and Parkomania

Many larger cities were quick to adapt Strauch's ideas in developing or reorganizing their cemeteries. By the beginning of the 1900s, the popularity of lawn parks, sometimes referred to as "parkomania," was widespread.

Although the designers of many lawn park cemeteries followed Strauch's concepts, they often ignored some of his most important lessons. Some allowed monuments that were large and ornate. This disrupted the principles of restraint and order. In other cases, overemphasis on open spaces and wide lawns threw off the careful balance between nature and human artistry.

Military Cemeteries

The nation's first military cemetery, Arlington National Cemetery, was created in 1864 at Arlington, Virginia. During the Civil War, Union (Northern) government officials grew increasingly concerned with the growing number of war casualties overflowing the hospitals and burial

Arlington National Cemetery in Arlington, Virginia, holds more than three hundred thousand graves. Any honorably discharged member of the U.S. armed forces is eligible for burial at Arlington.

grounds near Washington, D.C. The quartermaster general for the Union army, Montgomery Meigs, proposed that the government seize two hundred acres of Confederate (southern) general Robert E. Lee's family property, known as Arlington, to be used as a cemetery. The property had belonged to George Washington and was later inherited by Lee's wife, Washington's granddaughter. Meigs, angered by Lee's refusal to fight for Union forces, wanted to make sure that Lee and his family could never return to his estate.

By the war's end in 1865, sixteen thousand graves filled the spaces close to the house. At this time, the cemetery consisted of rows of unknown dead in ramshackle graves on a dirty field. Over time, the cemetery's 612 acres took on the form of a memorial lawn park, with its finely landscaped grounds and the simple white headstones that honor American soldiers from all wars.

Gettysburg

The Gettysburg National Cemetery in Gettysburg, Pennsylvania, was also established during the Civil War, following the North's victory in the bloody Battle of Gettysburg in 1863. It was created as a formal burial ground for dead Union soldiers, many of whom had been buried in small, shallow graves scattered throughout the area. The cemetery was dedicated by President Abraham Lincoln in

A crowd gathers around a seated President Lincoln at Gettysburg hours before he delivered his famous Gettysburg Address in an 1863 ceremony dedicating the national cemetery.

a ceremony just four months after the battle. During this ceremony, Lincoln delivered his famous Gettysburg Address. In it he spoke about the battle of Gettysburg and the reasons for fighting the war. He also honored the dead who lay buried there.

Confederate soldiers killed in that battle were not originally interred in the cemetery. It was not until 1870, five years after the Civil War had ended, that those soldiers were removed from other resting places and buried at Gettysburg. They were not the only other group to be buried there though. Military casualties from nearly every major American war have been brought to the cemetery. In the twenty-first century, Gettysburg contains the remains of thousands of soldiers from conflicts throughout American history.

The Presidio

The Presidio Park in San Francisco, California, is the home of the Presidio Cemetery, also known as the San Francisco National Cemetery. It was the first national military cemetery in the western United States. The U.S. Army took control of the land in 1846 from Mexico. A small cemetery already existed there. It contained remains of Mexican and Spanish soldiers. When the U.S. Army created its own cemetery in a different location in the park, it moved the Mexican and Spanish remains into unmarked graves. The first U.S. burials took place in 1854. Most of those buried in the cemetery were U.S. soldiers, but local civilians, including children, were also laid to rest there.

The cemetery grew rapidly soon after it was opened, but it was not well organized. Not until 1884, when the Presidio was officially designated a national cemetery, did officials started to keep records and number the graves. The cemetery was given several more acres of land, and the number of burials each year increased drastically.

In 1994 all military activities at the Presidio ceased. The National Park Service assumed oversight of the park and cemetery, which is open to the public.

The Punchbowl, officially called the National Memorial Cemetery of the Pacific, lies on the outskirts of downtown Honolulu, Hawaii.

The Punchbowl

One of the more unusual military cemeteries is found in an extinct volcano crater outside of Honolulu, Hawaii. This cemetery is known as the National Memorial Cemetery of the Pacific, or the Punchbowl. Long before it was transformed into a national cemetery, the area where the Punchbowl lies was used for human sacrifice by local tribes. The name *Punchbowl* is actually derived from the Hawaiian *puowaina,* which roughly translates to "hill of sacrifice."

The governor of Hawaii offered its use as a national cemetery in 1943, during World War II (1939–1945). It was dedicated in 1949, and its first burials took place during that year.

Since 1949 the U.S. government has made the Punchbowl cemetery a resting place for thousands of soldiers killed in World War II, the Korean War (1950–1953), and the Vietnam War (1957–1975). The Honolulu Memorial in the Punchbowl commemorates those who were lost at sea or who were missing in action during those wars.

I was somebody.
Who, is no business
of yours.
—ANONYMOUS GRAVESTONE, STOWE, VERMONT

CHAPTER FIVE

THE ISOLATION OF DEATH (1917–1949)

By the early 1900s, American attitudes toward death and burial had undergone vast changes. After the turn of the twentieth century, reformers concerned about land conservation and public health spoke out for cremation and urn burial. These burials take less land. Crematories sprang up in many major cities. Columbariums (vaults lined with recesses for urns) and community mausoleums were built in cemeteries to hold cremated remains.

The professional management of burials, which had started in the 1800s, continued to grow. Wakes, viewings (visiting the body before burial), and memorial services moved from the home to funeral parlors or cemeteries. Strangers, not family, buried the dead and maintained the grave site. These trends led to the development of the memorial park.

A columbarium contains small vaults to hold cremated remains. This columbarium is for the Neptune Society in San Francisco, California. The group started in the 1970s and is dedicated to promoting cremation.

"Silent Reminders of the Shortness of Life"

In 1915 cemetery designer J. J. Gordon wrote in the magazine *Cemetery Beautiful* that the ideal memorial park was an open space with no visible markers or monuments. Instead, markers laid flat into the ground would make death virtually undetectable.

In outlining his design, Gordon explained: "Few but have felt the chill that strikes the heart when standing in the office of some cemetery, even the most beautiful, and seeing the gleaming monuments, silent reminders of the shortness of life. [In the central memorial park] there is no note of sadness. The flowers fling their fragrance far and wide, the fountains tinkle merrily and it is a beautiful park and the onlooker enjoys it." This memorial garden solved many problems of cemetery design. For superintendents and maintenance crews, low-lying gravestones and monuments allowed for easier and faster mowing and landscaping. The plan was also democratic. In many cases, it would be harder to know the place in society of the deceased if most of the graves were similar.

Dr. Eaton's Vision

At about the same time, a former miner from Missouri, Hubert Eaton, took over the management of a failing cemetery in Los Angeles, California. According to legend, Hubert Eaton's vision for the cemetery came

to him in a flash on New Year's Day in 1917. While surveying the desolate grounds, he saw rising before his eyes "a great park, devoid of misshapen monuments and other customary signs of earthly death, but filled with towering trees, sweeping lawns, splashing fountains, singing birds, beautiful statuary, cheerful flowers, noble memorial architecture with interiors full of light and color . . . where artists study and sketch; where teachers bring happy children to see the things they read of in books, [like] objects of great art (in reproductions) and famous churches (in reconstructions)."

Eaton called his design for the cemetery Forest Lawn. He believed that earthly life was a joy and a wonder, and death was not to be feared. All who died were rewarded with a joyous life filled with everlasting sunshine and God's love. He was convinced that most cemeteries were depressing because they focused on death, grief, and loss. At Forest Lawn, he planned to eliminate the ugliness of death and to emphasize the beauty of life.

Hubert Eaton (*above*) had a vision for Forest Lawn. He wanted to make this cemetery in California a place of repose that focused on life.

New Form, Old Purpose

One of Eaton's goals with Forest Lawn was to lure people back to the cemetery. He thought that the public would respond to his ideal of life amid a landscape of the dead. To promote the cemetery, Eaton put up giant billboards all over Los Angeles. He advertised Forest Lawn as the "first step up toward Heaven." Another successful sales pitch was "Everything at the time of sorrow, in one sacred place, under one friendly management, with one convenient credit arrangement and a year to pay. ONE TELEPHONE CALL DOES EVERYTHING."

This is just one of the many billboards advertising Forest Lawn that could be seen around Los Angeles after Eaton took over as manager of the cemetery.

In Eaton's vocabulary, death became a mere "leave-taking," with no sense of finality about it. People who were remembered, Eaton reasoned, were never really gone. He also knew that the desire of people to be remembered forever was good for business. By playing on this desire, the sales staff at Forest Lawn might convince customers to spend money on more expensive caskets and on monuments that would endure for ages.

Eaton streamlined the process of burial, offering clients an array of packaged services to meet all needs, desires, and budgets. He pioneered the concept of prepayment for funeral and burial expenses, which he called the Before-Need Plan. He offered funeral packages to suit every budget. Cremation urns were available in a wide range of prices. The Olympus cost tens of thousands of dollars, while the Plastic Container and the Steel Box could be had for less than one hundred dollars.

Eaton saw to it that preparation for burial came with elaborate cosmetic treatment for the corpse so that the deceased looked "natural." Burial became "interment," and a grave was an "interment space." Later, Eaton employed grief counselors to help the bereaved overcome the sadness they felt at the death of a loved one.

Cemetery or Theme Park?

During the next several decades, thousands, both living and dead, passed through the largest wrought iron gates in the world to enter Forest Lawn Cemetery. To banish images of death from Forest Lawn, Eaton insisted that all artwork based on Christian themes—whether in the chapel or in any of the sections—portray a cheerful Jesus. "I wanted to erase all signs of mourning," he later said. Visitors found burial "gardens" with such names as "Inspiration Slope," "Sweet Memories," and "Dawn of Tomorrow," suggesting happiness, peace, rest, and hope. Young people had their own sections. The heart-shaped Babyland was designed for infant burials, and Slumberland was reserved for children and young adults.

Eaton also incorporated patriotic themes at Forest Lawn. They reflected the sense of optimism and triumph that he thought illustrated the American outlook on life. One area, known as the Court of Freedom, for example, contained a large mosaic that depicted the signing of the Declaration of Independence. A thirteen-foot-high statue of George Washington stood near it. By displaying great moments of the United States' past, Eaton encouraged people to recall happy times spent with loved ones rather than to dwell on the pain of their deaths.

This mosaic re-creation of the Signing of the Declaration of Independence by John Trumbull is three times the size of the famous original. It is just one of the patriotic reproductions found in the Court of Freedom at Forest Lawn.

When the technology became available, soothing music and inspirational messages floated out from speakers hidden in the shrubbery. Bronze markers installed flush to the ground identified the graves, adding to the "invisibility of the dead." One selling point of the markers was that over time they took on a greenish patina that made them appear to be a part of the lawn.

Eaton also stressed the prestige that came with burial near what he called Features. These are the reproductions of famous sculptures, such as Michelangelo's *David*, strategically located throughout the cemetery. Plots closest to a feature sold for more money and were reserved for the wealthiest patrons. As in the colonial burial ground, the location of a grave indicated the occupant's status in life. Many classic Hollywood stars are buried at Forest Lawn. Having a grave near Jimmy Stewart, Errol Flynn, or Humphrey Bogart granted greater importance to the deceased.

To emphasize the living rather than the dead, Eaton added wedding chapels to the cemetery. Forest Lawn has three nondenominational (for all religions) chapels—the Little Church of the Flowers, the Wee Kirk o' the Heather, and the Church of the Recessional. More than sixty thousand people have been married at Forest Lawn. More than two hundred and fifty thousand people are buried there.

Eaton realized that tourists wanted mementos and souvenirs to recall their visit to

The first couple to marry at the Little Church of the Flowers at Forest Lawn poses outside the chapel on their wedding day in 1923.

Two saleswomen stand behind counters waiting for customers at the first gift shop opened at Forest Lawn in the 1920s.

his cemetery. To satisfy them, he provided postcards, replicas of various features, and other assorted trinkets at the Forest Lawn gift shop. One of the more popular items on sale was a large plastic walnut with a label that read: "Forest Lawn Memorial-Park—in a Nutshell! Open me like a real nut . . . squeeze my sides or pry me open with a knife." Inside was a miniature booklet illustrated with scenes of the cemetery.

By the 1930s, Forest Lawn was a thriving enterprise. It was also one of the most popular tourist attractions in Los Angeles. Eaton eventually opened five other cemeteries in the area. But it was Forest Lawn that became the model of the twentieth-century cemetery. It combined the celebration of life with a keen sense of business, advertising, and profits. At the same time, it kept the unpleasantness of death in the background, safely out of sight and out of mind.

Adding to the appeal of the memorial park was its promise to include everyone regardless of class, color, or creed. The truth is, however, that Forest Lawn and its many imitators were rigidly segregated. Eaton flatly refused to bury blacks and other minorities in the same area as whites. He also insisted on burying members of the same religious denomination in their own sections. After World War II, Forest Lawn incorporated sections for veterans. These were usually distinguished by displays of U.S. flags and weaponry.

In spite of Forest Lawn's popularity, many people were appalled at the carnival-like atmosphere that Eaton promoted. They thought Eaton's

From the sky, Forest Lawn looks less like a cemetery than like a palatial estate. Because of the many flat stone markers, few gravestones are visible from the sky or the ground. Lush plantings give it an air of peace and tranquility.

commercialism was not only in bad taste but also unethical. It preyed on the bereaved at the time of their greatest weakness. Others thought that the American cemetery had lost its character as sacred ground. Still others were uncomfortable with the absence of death at Forest Lawn. It seemed to suggest that Americans could outwit death by hiding from it.

The Legacy of Forest Lawn

By the early part of the 2000s, Eaton's message has not changed much. The website for Forest Lawn reads:

> Imagine...in one afternoon you can see exact replicas of Michelangelo's greatest works such as *David*, *Moses*, and *La Pietà*;

Reproductions of many famous works of art line the walls of the Memorial Court of Honor at Forest Lawn. At the end of the hall is a stained glass reproduction of Leonardo da Vinci's *Last Supper*. Along the side walls are copies of Michelangelo's famous statues, including *La Pietà (second from left)*.

Leonardo da Vinci's immortal *Last Supper* re-created in brilliant stained glass; two of the world's largest paintings, *The Crucifix-ion* and *The Resurrection*; original bronze and marble statuary, rare coins, valuable 13th century stained glass, old world architecture; and much, much more. And in that same afternoon, you can even take a quiet stroll around a splashing fountain pond that's teeming with ducks and majestic swans! Best of all, it's free.

More than one million visitors stop at Forest Lawn each year, including thousands of schoolchildren on field trips. Eaton's contribution

This huge crowd gathered at Forest Lawn for an Easter celebration in the early 1920s.

to the history of cemeteries is questionable, however. His philosophy of "undertaking [preparing the dead for burial] . . . combined with all forms of interment in one sacred place, under one friendly management, with one convenient credit arrangement for everything" has underscored what many critics believed was the vulgar and heartless commercialization of death. For good or ill, Hubert Eaton linked death and profits. He made a business of dying.

*Traveler, someday when you arrive
in Kiev [Ukraine] tell that we,
faithful to the commandments
of our fatherland, are resting here.*

—UKRAINIAN AMERICAN GRAVESTONE

CHAPTER SIX

NEW LIQUID IN OLD VESSELS: ETHNIC CEMETERIES

The United States is a nation of immigrants. With each wave of immigration, new attitudes about death and burial have been introduced into U.S. society. From Day of the Dead ceremonies among Mexican Americans to the honoring of ancestors among Chinese Americans, cemeteries across the nation are reflecting new ways of understanding and dealing with death.

Bringing the Homeland to the United States

In the late 1800s and early 1900s, immigrants from eastern and southern Europe brought many of their ceremonies and practices for burying their dead to the United States. These burial rites were steeped in tradition and ritual. Whenever possible, immigrants established their own cemeteries. As one historian noted, "For immigrants, cemeteries fostered a sense of identity and stability in a new country characterized by change." Such cemeteries were also created out of need. Many cemetery managers kept out the new arrivals. They felt that immigrants had a "weird taste . . . for freakish monuments and such."

On the Great Plains, immigrant cemeteries were established beyond the town limits so they would be more easily accessible to those who lived on outlying farms. Many of these cemeteries started out as single-family plots. Over time they grew to include members of the entire community. As overcrowding threatened these cemeteries, immigrant communities might also create cemetery associations to raise funds to buy additional land.

The cemeteries created by immigrants shared certain characteristics. They were often placed on the highest point of land so as to be closer to heaven. The highest sites also provided better drainage. Immigrant cemeteries on the prairie, where hills were scarce, faced a different kind of challenge. Czech and other eastern European immigrants in Nebraska, for example, solved the problem by building a stone wall, filling it in with dirt, and creating a cemetery on top.

A fence of painted wood, stone, or elegant wrought iron with a fancy entrance gate often enclosed immigrant cemeteries. Headstones and markers were made with improvised materials. Since there was little available stone on the prairie, people used concrete or metal, including wrought iron or zinc crosses, to mark their grave sites. Less often, the immigrants used wooden markers.

Whenever possible, trees or flowers common to the immigrants' homeland were planted on grave sites. In some Czech cemeteries on the Great Plains, for example, tiger lilies and lilacs, popular plantings of this period, were placed on or behind the grave. The immigrant settlers planted tall evergreens such as Austrian pine, blue spruce, or red cedar at the four corners of a family plot or a cemetery. The trees reminded the immigrants of the great forests in Europe. They also served as markers to make it easier to locate a cemetery on the flat prairie, where there were few trees. The slow growth of trees and their long lives symbolized the commitment of the community to their dead.

In Memory Of

Immigrant cemeteries did not follow a particular American cemetery design. Some ethnic communities designed cemeteries that had features of rural cemeteries, though they were much simpler in plan. Mostly, though, immigrant cemeteries reflected the cemeteries in the country

Immigrants built cemeteries in the traditions of their homelands. This Czech cemetery in Alabama has large monuments and walled burial plots.

of origin—whether it was in Czechoslovakia (present-day Czech Republic and Slovakia), Poland, Russia, Greece, or Italy. The cemeteries helped immigrants hold onto some of their cultural traditions while facing the challenges of American society.

For many immigrants, the most important part of the burial plot was the headstone. Many immigrant cemeteries contain large headstones and monuments that dominate the landscape. Like the earlier European immigrants to the Americas, later immigrants believed that a large and distinctive monument better reflected the family's status within the community.

In Ukrainian cemeteries, markers were made of stone. Some had very simple inscriptions in Ukrainian. They gave the deceased's birth and death dates and town of origin. Often the deceased's last name, translated into the Roman alphabet, was carved on the back of the marker. Others had Ukrainian phrases or symbols, patterns from folk art, political symbols, or images of Ukrainian shrines. One gravestone in a Ukrainian cemetery in Pennsylvania has an image of Cossacks, the historic warriors of Ukraine.

For Italian immigrants, the cemetery was an important connection between the land of the living and the dead. Italian graves, often decorated with flowers and plantings, were enclosed by miniature fences. The fence kept out animals and human feet. It also maintained the grave site as separate and distinct from others surrounding it.

Grave markers in Italian American cemeteries were either homemade or, if the family could afford it, carved out of stone. Christian religious symbols, such as a cross, sometimes were carved into the grave marker. The site might also contain a small statue representing a patron saint. Personal mementos such as religious medals, photos, articles of clothing, or objects used by the deceased were laid about the grave—not only as a reminder for the family but to show outsiders a life once lived.

One distinctive aspect of the Italian American cemeteries is the ceramic photo images imbedded into memorial stones. These first appeared in the late 1800s and early 1900s. They continued in use until the 1940s. For families that could not afford an expensive carved memorial, these ceramic photos offered another way to commemorate a dead relative.

At first, these photo memorials were rejected by memorial parks. The parks felt that the photo stones did not fit with the scenic nature of the grounds. One writer commented that it was good that few Italian Americans could afford such stone portraits. He stated that if "there was much of this, our burial grounds would become ghostly indeed." Those who appreciated the practice, however, saw something else. Another writer noted that the photographic portrait was "not merely the likeness" of the deceased. It was "*the very shadow of the person lying there fixed forever!*" These memorials became a staple in the cemeteries of other ethnic groups from eastern and southern Europe, no matter what their religion.

Photo memorials on gravestones became popular in the Italian immigrant community. This stone is in New Hradec, North Dakota.

Honoring the Jewish Memory

During the colonial period, some Jews were buried in the community cemetery. Later, Jewish Americans created their own burial grounds. Hebrew letters and special symbols such as the Star of David and broken flowers adorned the gravestones. Often clumsily carved by local non-Jewish stonecutters, the markers might contain mistakes in spelling that garbled the meanings of the Hebrew language.

In Jewish cemeteries, inscriptions often appear in Hebrew as well as English.

By the late 1800s, as some Jews sought to assimilate into U.S. society, they began borrowing decorative themes from Christian cemeteries. The result was Jewish burial grounds filled with a mixture of traditions. There might be ornate urns, Greek columns, and Roman statuary intermixed with more traditional markers in Hebrew. Many Jewish death dates are inscribed according to the Jewish calendar, which predates the Christian calendar by three thousand years. One Jewish custom is to place small, loose pebbles at the grave site to show respect for the dead.

Preserving Cultural Practices

Twenty-first-century cemeteries work closely with ethnic groups to make sure that cultural traditions are preserved and respected. For Chinese Americans, some cemeteries provide a feng shui expert to choose a grave site that will receive positive spiritual energy. This might mean placing a family plot near water or a mountain.

In California, cemeteries have built rooms where Hindu families can wash their deceased with honey and yogurt before cremations. They also provide special pots for Vietnamese families in which to burn the paper money their ancestors need in the afterlife. Some cemeteries—especially memorial parks—have changed their policies to allow visitors to leave stones on Jewish grave sites. Russian Jews are allowed to burn a heavy, strong incense for their dead. At one California cemetery, perishable

Mourners at this Chinese cemetery in Hawaii leave behind food offerings for their deceased relatives.

grave offerings such as fruit (a Chinese custom) and pork (a Pacific Island custom) are permitted. Cemetery officials reserve the right to remove the offerings before they rot.

When designing new burial areas, cemetery managers consider cultural preferences. For instance, a garden area might be designed specifically for the flat monuments preferred by Latino and Filipino families. Another might incorporate vaults for those who want to bury cremation urns.

Some cemeteries allow important cultural celebrations. For example, the Mexican *Día de los Muertos* (Day of the Dead) is held on the first and second days of November. Mexican American families go to the cemetery

Many Mexican Americans celebrate *Día de los Muertos* every November. The celebration honors the dead and can involve eloborate displays, like this one at a California cemetery.

to visit, picnic, and celebrate the lives of their deceased family members. On the Chinese *Ching Ming*, the day for ancestor worship, calligraphers write family names on strips of yellow paper and mourners burn stacks of paper money. The cemetery might set up an offering table for the dead and provide a buffet for the living. Members of a Buddhist temple, dressed in yellow robes, might hold a chanting ceremony.

Commercial cemeteries are facing decreasing membership. Families that once preferred plots and mausoleums are increasingly choosing simpler options such as simple wood coffins or cremation. Attracting new customers is smart business, so commercial cemeteries are sending messages of multiculturalism across the country. Families from other cultures often still choose lavish burial arrangements, which can start at as much as ten thousand dollars. For cemeteries this adds a needed source of revenue. For some ethnic groups, this new approach provides a way to honor their dead loved ones without making a costly trip back to a homeland to bury them.

The evolution of ethnic cemeteries and the assimilation of various ethnic groups into once-white-European-only cemeteries has bene-fited the cultural landscape of the United States. It provides different ways of looking at the universal experience of death. It also gives peo-ple another way of understanding the changing nature of their history, values, and beliefs.

CHAPTER SEVEN

THE CHANGING FACE OF DEATH (1960–PRESENT)

The arrival of the memorial park cemetery in the early 1900s promoted a model that is still used throughout the nation. Hubert Eaton's design was meant to bring back memories of the rural cemeteries of the 1800s. But it really was more an extension of the lawn park design. The memorial park marked a final shift in Americans' attitudes toward death. The care of the dead, once a family responsibility, was turned over to funeral directors, florists, cemetery superintendents, and cemetery maintenance workers.

In the 1960s, cemeteries had become places of isolation and desolation. Busier lives meant fewer people visited, even on weekends and holidays. Other than memorial parks, which offered other attractions, cemeteries were silent, sterile cities of the dead.

The annual death rate in the United States began to decrease dramatically after 1900. Improved health care, sanitation, and diet helped people live longer. The death rate of infants went from 162.4 per 1,000 in 1900 to 23.1 in 1966. At the beginning of the twenty-first century, the death rate for infants was 6.3 per 1,000. For adults during the same period, the death rate went from 17.2 per 1,000 in 1900 to 9.2 in 1966. By the early 2000s, the death rate had decreased to approximately 8.3 per 1,000. Americans were living longer. Death seemed farther away than ever.

The Business of Grief

As the death rate decreased, burial business opportunities decreased. Cemeteries had to compete with one another for business. Beginning in the 1960s, corporations began buying up local cemeteries to develop statewide, regional, and national networks. These large companies provided everything: burial lots, cremation niches, burial vaults, caskets, grave markers, and services.

Although state boards regulate the licensing of cemeteries and monitor public health concerns, cemeteries generally operate with few restrictions. This freedom does not mean that cemeteries are always competent and honest. Jessica Mitford wrote a book in the 1960s exposing the commercialism of the funeral business. In it she says of funeral directors, "To be 'ethical' merely means to adhere to a prevailing code of morality, in this case one devised over the years by the undertakers themselves for their own purposes."

Abuses in business include sloppy bookkeeping and the theft of funds set aside for cemetery and grave maintenance. In some cases, remains have been removed from plots, the ashes of cremated bodies have been mixed up, bodies were not cremated in a timely fashion, and more than one body was buried in a single grave to save space.

Even so, the death-care industry continues to be successful. The nation's largest holding company of funeral homes and cemeteries, Service Corporation International (SCI), has hundreds of funeral homes and

Investigators search for remains of bodies left neglected on the property of a crematorium in Georgia.

cemeteries in twenty-five states and five Canadian provinces. The founder of SCI, Robert Waltrip, told *Business Week* that he hoped to turn his company into the "Tru-Value hardware of the funeral service industry." By 2000 cemeteries were making a profit of almost $12 billion a year, while performing more than two million funerals and burials annually.

Green Options

The American population is aging. Seventy-seven million Americans will turn fifty years old between 1996 and 2015. The death rate will rise as more people grow older. Standardization in burials and cemetery plots has become the norm. Yet many Americans are looking for alternatives that are more personal and often cheaper.

One of the popular alternatives in the twenty-first century in the United States is the green burial. This is an environmentally friendly philosophy for burying the dead. In a green burial, a family wraps the corpse in a shroud or places it in a bio-degradable box of unfinished wood. In some cases, the body is not covered at all. Often graves are dug by hand using only shovels. The bodies are not embalmed. There are no burial vaults or plastic flowers. Some graves are unmarked, while others have small, flat, inscribed stones. In some cases, dead pets might be buried with the deceased.

Some cemeteries have taken note of this trend and have acquired land that is "nature-friendly" for green burials. These areas are relatively untouched. They do not have expensive landscaping or maintained lawns. Some of these cemeteries have put in hiking and walking trails so people can relax with nature and their loved ones. Other cemeteries are considering offering the green grounds for other occasions too. These might include weddings or even art classes.

Green burials are also a way for the dead to make a political statement about the environment from their graves. George Russell was pleased that the green burial of his mother Marjorie Russell in 2007 would benefit all living things. He wrote: "Her life is a perpetual legacy to the

Green cemeteries, such as this one in Colorado, are becoming increasingly popular.

future of, not only Texas and the U.S., but to the entire biosphere that keeps us all alive."

Many environmentalists support the green movement because they believe that cemeteries harm the environment by using toxic fertilizers or pesticides to maintain the landscape. They also endanger humans by exposing people and the ground to deadly embalming chemicals. As one green cemetery owner described the practice, the dead "will re-nurture the circle of life, fertilize the soil and provide a perpetual legacy to beauty. It doesn't make sense to destroy rain forests by making mahogany coffins, or even worse turn the person into a toxic pickle." But even for those who are not driven by environmental concerns, the green burial movement with its low costs and appealing setting is an attractive option.

More Americans are turning to cremation as another cost-cutting and environmentally friendly way to handle the dead. The number of people

In cremation the body is placed in a high-temperature retort *(above)* and burned to ashes. The process costs less than traditional burial methods of preserving the body and burying it in a casket.

choosing cremation has risen dramatically from 6 percent of the deceased in 1975 to over 30 percent in the early twenty-first century. People can pay as much or as little for a cremation as they desire, depending on the type of service they choose.

The Sky's the Limit

Many people are looking for new ways to honor the ashes of their loved ones besides placing them in an urn or vault. Some families scatter ashes of the deceased over water or across a special piece of land. Other creative options are available too. For a fee, the ashes, or cremains, are mixed with concrete and molded into "reef balls." These balls are planted underwater by divers. There they become habitats for ocean coral, sponges, and fish. Some reef balls are placed in concrete cemetery grottoes, or concrete reefs, which serve as larger habitats for sea life.

A family might place the cremains in a large helium balloon that rises as high as five miles above the earth. The balloon freezes in the cold air at that height, and the cremains are scattered from it. One relatively new approach is for cremains to travel to outer space. The ashes, contained in lipstick-size containers, orbit Earth for almost a decade before burning up.

Some other unusual memorials have included putting the cremains in

A worker lowers an artificial reef created from human remains mixed with cement into the Gulf of Mexico.

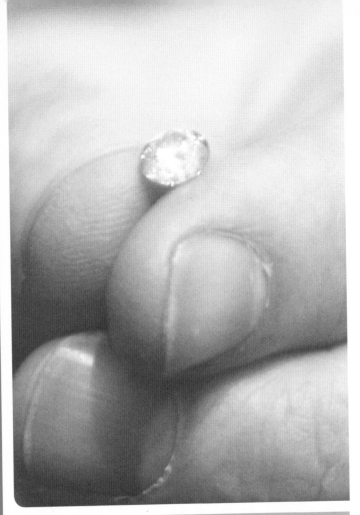

This synthetic 1.32 carat diamond was created from human ashes at LifeGem in Saint Louis, Missouri.

the clay that is used to make special pieces of commemorative bone china. Or the ashes might be absorbed into paint to create a piece of art. For twenty thousand dollars, a person's cremains can be pressed into a one carat LifeGem diamond that the family can display.

Pet Cemeteries

For many, the loss of a beloved pet finds them making funeral arrangements at one of the many pet cemeteries in the United States. The idea of a pet cemetery is more than a century old. In 1896 a prominent New York veterinarian, Dr. Samuel Johnson, offered his apple orchard in then-rural Hartsdale, New York, as a burial site for a friend's dog. Johnson's idea caught on. A number of pet cemeteries were established that offered caskets, plots, or cremation and simple funeral services for the deceased pet's family. Quite often the grounds and monuments in these special resting places are equal to those in human burial grounds. But unlike human cemeteries, where there is little interaction among mourners, pet cemeteries have a way of bringing people together to talk about and mourn their pets. One of the more famous pet cemeteries is Pet's Rest outside of San Francisco, California. The cemetery is the final resting place for more than thirteen thousand pets, including dogs, cats, birds, monkeys, exotic animals, and goldfish.

Death and the Computer Age

To stay competitive, cemeteries throughout the country are using computer technology. Computers are set up to keep records and to manage accounts. They are also used to offer new services to customers. Some cemeteries supply ATMs for those in need of quick cash. With the help of computers, granite for tombstones can come in many colors, either polished or rough. It can be laser cut into a variety of shapes, including hearts, cubes, and crosses. Photographs, family genealogy diagrams, symbols of the deceased's hobbies and profession, images of pets, or favorite objects can be laser etched, hand chiseled, mounted on, or sandblasted into the stone.

Computer technology has also been used to design glow-in-the-dark tombstones and talking tombstones. A visitor presses a button on the grave marker and hears the recorded voice of the deceased. Among the newest offerings are video biographies of the dead stored in cemetery kiosks. Visitors can enter any kiosk that has a computer screen. When they log on, they hear the gentle strains of music and a voice that welcomes them. Then a video biography of the deceased appears from the cemetery's online archive.

More than thirteen thousand pets are buried at Pet's Rest Cemetery in Colma, California.

Cemeteries that use this new technology also make the video biographies available for downloading to a home computer. Some cemeteries have websites that allow people to record their own biographies for later use. Video biographies have become the twenty-first-century version of the monument or mausoleum found in the rural cemeteries of the 1800s. According to the cemetery owner who pioneered the concept, people needed a change. "I saw that the traditional forms did not serve the purpose of the community. A priest or member of the community reading a few words didn't do enough. . . . Art and death have always had a strong connection, and art emerged as the answer."

One man, who had lost his six-year-old son, sees the videos as helpful. "Something like this will not be erased," he stated. "Everywhere I go I can see it on the Internet. My grandchildren and great-grandchildren will see it. I will be able to say, 'That was your uncle, your cousin.'" Some

This thirty-six-ton granite memorial Mercedes-Benz tops the grave of Ray Tse Jr. His brother commissioned the scupture for Ray's plot at Rosehill Cemetery in Linden, New Jersey.

traditionalists, however, find the videos disrespectful of the dead. They believe the availability of these mini-documentaries, which can be viewed by anyone, is a violation of a family's privacy.

Letting Go

Although video biographies and personalized gravestones help many families cope with their grief, others see a disturbing trend. Critics, including some religious scholars and clergy, are disturbed by this practice of "customizing" death. They feel that it lessens the spiritual significance of cemeteries. Many point out that the popularity of these practices shows a desire of Americans to build shrines to themselves, rather than reflect on spiritual destiny.

Supporters of new technology and the trends in burial memorials argue that customizing death helps preserve a connection to the living. It also shows outsiders that this life was important to someone. Some cemetery owners say that no matter what the burials may involve, the rituals offer comfort and peace to the bereaved.

Circumstances Led Me to This End

—LATE NINETEENTH-CENTURY EPITAPH

EPILOGUE

SAVING THE AMERICAN CEMETERY (1960–PRESENT)

Benjamin Franklin once said, "Show me your cemeteries, and I will tell you what kind of people you have." In earlier times, cemeteries showed a society respectful of its dead. By the twenty-first century, older cemeteries are no longer viewed in sacred terms. Many are being destroyed to make way for new developments such as shopping malls and housing. To remind people of the important historic and cultural role that cemeteries have played, a movement to protect and preserve these cemeteries has emerged throughout the nation.

Abandoning the Dead

Cemeteries have always been the targets of grave robbers searching for valuables or, in some cases, bodies for medical school classes. Relic hunters dig up the graves of soldiers to retrieve military paraphernalia to sell on the collectors' market.

Incidents of cemetery vandalism have increased dramatically in the United States. Some are hate crimes, such as the desecration of Jewish cemeteries. Some are plain acts of vandalism, such as breaking tombstones and tearing up plantings. Cemetery ornaments are often stolen to adorn someone's backyard or are bought and sold through collectors and auctions. Cemeteries once offered solace and quiet. In the modern world, Americans tend to visit cemeteries in groups during the day to avoid being robbed or worse.

Souls of the Lost

Older graveyards and cemeteries are in danger of disappearing because of the destructive effects of weather and pollution, as well as urban

Cemeteries are sometimes the target for vandals. This Jewish cemetery, Adath Chesed Shel Emes Cemetery in Crystal, Minnesota, was desecrated in the early 1990s.

This marker indicates the grave of Nancy Barnett. When county officials wanted to move her grave in 2003, her grandson protested and the road was built around it.

and suburban growth. The spread of shopping centers, new subdivisions, and roadways regularly threaten cemeteries, both visible and forgotten. For instance, in 2000 a highway expansion project meant the removal of the remains of 3 early settlers from the community of Toncray, Virginia. That same year, 35 Civil War-era yellow-fever victims in Wilmington, North Carolina, were dug up from an abandoned graveyard. Workers at the Saint Louis, Missouri, airport removed more than 9,550 bodies from a nearby hillside cemetery to expand its runways. In all cases, the bodies were moved to another burial ground.

To make room for the necessities of suburban living, more developers are digging up and moving graves. Opposition to grave removals can be fierce, particularly when descendants of the dead become involved. In many areas, local activists battle improvement plans that pose any kind of threat to older burial grounds. Some argue that a skeleton must disintegrate entirely before the deceased's spiritual journey is considered complete. As one cemetery preservationist remarked, "It's not acceptable to think of our ancestors being moved simply because it's more convenient for a developer." Still, many people, when faced with the possibility of a grave being buried under tons of concrete and iron, or moved, prefer to have the remains removed.

Archaeological assistants dig up a child's grave in Montgomeryville, Pennsylvania. It is one of 250 graves being relocated from a busy intersection.

Some developers are showing more sensitivity to the concerns of the public and are considering ways to incorporate existing cemeteries into the new landscaping plans. In 2000, for example, the University of Rhode Island debated moving the remains of an eighteenth-century family to make way for a new building on campus. Instead, the school decided to work around the site by walling it off and adding a memorial tree. Sometimes retail developers add green space with small trees and plantings to mark a burial site.

Abandoned Cemeteries

Abandoned cemeteries are another problem, particularly in the South. There, backyard burials were once typical. Archaeologists, historians, and preservationists scramble to document these cemeteries before they disappear. More than ten thousand abandoned cemeteries have been identified in North Carolina since the 1990s. That figure is probably just a fraction of the total number of cemeteries that once existed. Many believe that the same holds true for the states of South Carolina, Virginia, and Georgia.

Preserving the Past—Preserving the Dead

Activists are calling attention to the plight of many older and endangered American burial grounds. Americans, especially those who live in large cities, have once more come to regard cemeteries as a pleasant green space in which to walk, jog, ride bicycles, or find a quiet place to reflect during the day. Historic cemeteries have opened their grounds to host activities including weddings, campouts, picnics, concerts, and even small carnivals. Funds raised by these events help the cemeteries to maintain the grounds and make needed repairs.

While U.S. laws do not protect American cemeteries, many state, local, and private organizations have pushed for laws to do so. The National Park Service and the Preservation for the National Trust have special programs that deal specifically with the preservation of cemeteries. Many historic cemeteries have been listed on the National Register of Historic Places. This listing offers some protection from destruction. Genealogy societies, collecting information about ancestors, work with other groups or families to try to protect their graves.

In 2005 Hurricane Katrina devastated New Orleans, including many of the historic aboveground cemeteries. Four of the five cemeteries on the National Register of Historic Places were flooded for over two weeks. The storm damaged sculptures and wrought iron fences and gates. It weakened bricks and mortar. A group called Save Our Cemeteries had overseen preservation of these cemeteries for a number of years. Since Katrina, Save Our Cemeteries has been working with the Federal Emergency Management Agency (FEMA), the City of New Orleans, and the local Catholic churches to evaluate the damage from wind and water and to seek funds to make the needed repairs.

The key to saving American cemeteries is educating the public. Interested groups have created books, magazines, newsletters, and Internet sites to pass on information and resources. Genealogy organizations have been instrumental in raising awareness of the plight of historic cemeteries. Schools are learning to use cemeteries to teach schoolchildren about local history. Students at some colleges and universities can study the history and art of cemeteries and their role in American culture and society.

"The Last Great Necessity"

As resting places for the dead, cemeteries are mirrors to the living. They reflect our religious beliefs, morality, and sense of beauty.

A cemetery presents, an anonymous poet notes, "a history of people—a perpetual record of yesterday

Hurricane Katrina flooded many of the aboveground cemeteries in New Orleans in 2005. This coffin was dislodged, along with many others.

and sanctuary of peace and quiet today. . . . A cemetery exists," the poet continues, "because every life is worth loving and remembering—always." As U.S. citizens, we can contemplate these words as well as those of Benjamin Franklin to discover what sort of people we are and what sort we may wish to become.

Holy Sepulchre Cemetery, located in Omaha, Nebraska, is just one of many ethnic cemeteries found in the city. Before the opening of Holy Sepulchre Cemetery, many Catholics were buried at Cassedy's Burial Ground, a nonsectarian (for all religions) cemetery. Beginning in 1873, however, Cassedy's was closed to Catholics, following the decree of the First Council of Baltimore. It forbade Catholics from being buried in such a cemetery when a Catholic cemetery was available.

Immigrants to the United States often marked their graves in their native languages. This gravestone (above) is in Italian. Immigrants also used familiar symbols, such as the Irish Celtic cross (left).

The cemetery has historically served as a final resting place for American Roman Catholics of Irish and Italian descent. The grounds—with their gently winding roads, sloping landscaped lawns, and trees and bushes—are reminiscent of both a park cemetery and a rural cemetery. The monuments range in size from large decorated mausoleums to small rocklike markers.

The cemetery is also interesting for its layout. To the east of the main road, Irish American markers predominate. To the west are the Italian American graves. Irish graves such as the one pictured in the lower right on the opposite page feature a Celtic cross, a strong Irish-Catholic religious symbol. Italian graves such these on the upper left and right hand pages range from simple markers with a family name and ceramic photos of the deceased. Inscriptions were often in both Italian and English. Markers also feature mementos left in honor of the deceased *(below)*.

Italian Americans often placed photos of the deceased on the gravestones *(above)*. Many cultures, including the Irish, leave mementos on gravestones in honor of the deceased *(below)*.

TIMELINE

3000 B.C.–A.D. 1500 Mound burials are common among Native Americans.

A.D. 700 Native Americans in the Mississippi Valley begin building effigy mounds.

1100 The Serpent Mount of the Adena culture, one of the most well-preserved effigy mounds, is built in Ohio.

1712 The Common Burial Ground, for slaves and free blacks, is established in Newport, Rhode Island.

1718 The city of New Orleans is founded.

1789 The Saint Louis Cemetery #1 is founded in New Orleans as the city's first aboveground cemetery.

1796 James Hillhouse founds the New Burying Ground Society in New Haven, Connecticut. The society establishes the New Burying Ground, later renamed the Grove Street Cemetery, that same year.

1832 Mount Auburn Cemetery, the first American rural cemetery, opens in Boston, Massachusetts.

1855 Adolphe Strauch redesigns Spring Grove cemetery in Cincinnati, Ohio.

1857 Frederick Law Olmsted designs Central Park in New York City, using elements and ideas from rural cemeteries.

1861 The Civil War begins in the United States.

1863 The Gettysburg National Cemetery is established in Gettysburg, Pennsylvania.

1864 Arlington National Cemetery, the first military cemetery in the United States, is founded in Arlington, Virginia.

1884   Presidio Park, in San Francisco, California, is officially
       designated a national cemetery.

1887   The Association of American Cemetery
       Superintendents (AACS) is founded.

1896   Samuel Johnson buries a friend's dog in his apple
       orchard, creating the first American pet cemetery.

1915   Cemetery designer J. J. Gordon proposes a new kind of
       memorial park, without visible markers or monuments,
       in the magazine *Cemetery Beautiful*.

1917   Hubert Eaton radically redesigns Forest Lawn cemetery
       in Los Angeles, California.

1949   The National Memorial Cemetery of the Pacific, also
       known as the Punchbowl, is dedicated.

1962   Service Corporation International (SCI), currently
       the largest holding company of funeral homes and
       cemeteries in the United States, is founded by Robert
       L. Waltrip.

2005   Hurricane Katrina devastates New Orleans and severely
       damages many of its aboveground cemeteries.

Arlington National Cemetery

Arlington, Virginia

(703) 607-8000

http://www.arlingtoncemetery.org/

More than three hundred thousand people are interred in the nation's second-largest military cemetery, including President John F. Kennedy, the crew of the space shuttle *Challenger*, and veterans of every war in the history of the United States.

Colma, California

http://www.colma.ca.gov/

The small town of Colma is notable for being a city where the dead outnumber the living. With seventeen cemeteries—and one pet cemetery— there are thousands of dead people for every living person in Colma. In 1900, San Francisco, only a few miles to the north, outlawed the construction of any more cemeteries in the crowded city and in 1912 decreed that all the existing cemeteries had to be moved outside the city limits. Those cemeteries were moved to Colma, and 73 percent of the town is occupied by cemeteries. Famous people interred here include newspaper owner William Randolph Hearst, baseball player Joe DiMaggio, and gunslinger Wyatt Earp.

Forest Lawn Cemetery

Los Angeles, California

(800) 204-3131

http://www.forestlawn.com/

Forest Lawn was redesigned by Hubert Eaton in 1917 to emphasize the living, not the dead. The park's many attractions—including reproductions of famous statues and paintings, wedding chapels, and a gift shop—have made it extraordinarily popular but have also led many to call it a theme park, rather than a cemetery. Whatever your opinion, this enormous cemetery is still worth the trip.

Fort Snelling National Cemetery

Minneapolis, Minnesota

(612) 726-1127

http://www.cem.va.gov/CEM/cems/nchp/ftsnelling.asp

Though this cemetery was dedicated in 1939, the remains from the original Fort Snelling, established in 1805, were transferred here. The interred in Fort Snelling are notable Minnesotans and military personnel. The fort itself has been restored to resemble its original appearance and is now an educational attraction.

Gettysburg National Military Park

Gettysburg, Pennsylvania

(717) 334-1124, ext. 431

http://www.nps.gov/getc/index.htm

Famous for being the site of Abraham Lincoln's 1863 Gettysburg Address, the Gettysburg cemetery was founded to house the Union dead from the Battle of Gettysburg—more than three thousand men. The cemetery is now part of the larger military park, which includes numerous monuments, a visitor's center, and preserved, undeveloped sections of the original battlefield.

Great Serpent Mound

Adams County, Ohio

(937) 587-2796

http://ohsweb.ohiohistory.org/places/sw16/index.shtml

This effigy mound, the largest in the world, is not technically a burial site—no human remains have been found here. Nevertheless, it is a fascinating site to visit. The mound stretches nearly a quarter of a mile from one end to the other and is more than three thousand years old. The Ohio Historical Society has a museum near the site, and a pathway extends around the entire mound.

Key West Cemetery

Key West, Florida

(305) 292-8177

http://www.keywest.com/cemetery.html

This aboveground cemetery is notable for its large number of unique and interesting tombstones, including one shaped like a ship's mast and one that simply says "I Told You I Was Sick." One grave, of a man who was a soldier in the War of 1812 (1812–1815) and a privateer, says that he was a "good citizen for 65 of his 108 years."

Mikveh Israel Cemetery

Philadelphia, Pennsylvania

(215) 922-5446

http://www.mikvehisrael.org/TheCemeteries/

The second-largest Jewish cemetery in the United States, Mikveh Israel holds the remains of many distinguished early Americans and is a national historic site. Among those buried here is Haym Salomon, a personal friend of George Washington and financier of the Revolutionary War. He was captured and sentenced to death by the British but managed to escape. Tours are available by appointment.

National Memorial Cemetery of the Pacific

Honolulu, Hawaii

(808) 532-3720

http://www.cem.va.gov/CEM/cems/nchp/nmcp.asp

This cemetery, located in the crater of an extinct volcano, holds the remains of more than thirty-four thousand veterans of World War I, World War II, the Korean War, and the Vietnam War. The Honolulu Memorial in the cemetery honors military personnel who are missing in action or lost or buried at sea in the Pacific Ocean.

New Orleans, Louisiana

http://www.neworleansonline.com/

New Orleans has forty-two cemeteries featuring elaborate statues, vaults, and ornate crypts. Many of them also offer guided tours. Saint Louis Cemetery #1 features the tomb of Marie Laveau, known as the Voodoo Queen. Legend has it that if you draw three *x*'s on her tomb, her spirit will grant you a wish.

Spring Grove Cemetery

Cincinnati, Ohio

(513) 681-7526

http://www.springgrove.org/

The original garden cemetery was founded in 1844, drawing inspiration from Mount Auburn, near Boston, Massachusetts, and the famous Père Lachaise cemetery in Paris, France. Among those buried at Spring Grove are forty Civil War generals. Spring Grove is also known for the extensive collection of both native and exotic trees on the grounds.

Trinity Church

New York City, New York

(212) 368-1600

http://www.trinitywallstreet.org/welcome/?cemetery

The only remaining active cemetery on the island of Manhattan, Trinity Church Cemetery houses the remains of many famous New Yorkers, including artists, soldiers, and politicians.

SOURCE NOTES

6   Margaret M. Coffin, *Death in Early America* (New York: Elsevier / Nelson Books, 1976), 228.

16   Lynn Rainville, *African American Cemeteries in Albemarle and Amherst Counties*, 2007, http://www.virginia.edu/woodson/projects/aacaac/index .shtml (October 17, 2007).

17   Elliott J. Gorn, "Black Spirits: The Ghostlore of Afro-American Slaves," *American Quarterly*, 36, no. 4 (Autumn 1984): 549–565.

18   Hansen, Joyce and Gary McGowan, *Breaking Ground, Breaking Silence* (New York: Henry Holt, 1998), 36

22   Michael Bathrick, "The 'Lulu' Carver of Richmond, MA," *BerkshireWeb*, n.d., http://www.berkshireweb.com/plexus/graveyards/rip.html (October 17, 2007).

24   New York Correction History Society, "City Cemetery, Hart Island (Potter's Field)," *City of New York Department of Corrections*, n.d., http://www .correctionhistory.org/html/chronicl/nycdoc/html/hart.html#Origin (October 17, 2007).

25   David E. Stannard, "Calm Dwellings," *American Heritage*, August/September 1979, 43.

25   David Charles Sloane, *The Last Great Necessity: Cemeteries in American History* (Baltimore, MD: Johns Hopkins University Press, 1991), 30.

29   Caroline F. Orne, *Sweet Auburn and Mount Auburn with Other Poems*, Cambridge, MA: John Owen, 1844.

30   Sloane, *The Last Great Necessity,* 43.

32   Lydia Maria Child, *The Mother's Book* (Boston: Carter and Hendee, 1831), 81.

34   Blanche Linden-Ward, "Strange but Genteel Pleasure Grounds: Tourist and Leisure Uses of Nineteenth-Century Rural Cemeteries," In Richard E. Meyer, ed., *Cemeteries and Gravemarkers: Voices of American Culture* (Ann Arbor, MI: U.M.I. Research Press, 1989), 305.

34   Harriet Martineau, *Retrospect of Western Travel*, (Armonk, NY: M. E. Sharpe, 2000), 227.

34 Emily Dickinson, "Letter from Emily Dickinson to a Schoolfriend, September 8, 1846," in Thomas H. Johnson, ed., *Emily Dickinson: Selected Letters* (Cambridge, MA: Belknap Press, 1971), 7–8.

36 Sloane, David Charles, *The Last Great Necessity* (Baltimore and London: The Johns Hopkins University Press, 1991), 55–56.

40 Stannard, "Calm Dwellings," 54.

42 Coffin, *Death in Early America,* 229.

43 Sloane, *The Last Great Necessity*, 100.

43 Blanche Linden-Ward and David Charles Sloane, "Spring Grove: The Founding of Cincinnati's Rural Cemetery, 1845–55," *Queen City Heritage* 43 (Spring 1985): 29–30.

44 Sloane, *The Last Great Necessity,* 103.

44 Richard Morris, *Sinners, Lovers, and Heroes: An Essay on Memorializing in Three American Cultures* (Albany, NY: SUNY Press, 1997), 147–148.

45 Ibid., 148.

45 James Farrell, *Inventing the American Way of Death 1830–1920* (Philadelphia: Temple University Press, 1980), 120.

45 Ibid,, 118.

45 Sloane, *The Last Great Necessity*, 105.

47 Cedar Hill Cemetery, "Jacob Weidenmann," *Cedar Hill Cemetery and Foundation*, 2005, http://www.cedarhillcemetery.org/Weidenmann.htm (March 20, 2007).

53 June Shaputis, "Funny Stones to Tickle Your Funny Bones," *Webpanda .com*, 1998, http://www.webpanda.com/ponder/epitaphs.htm (October 17, 2007).

54 J. J. Gordon, "The Ideal Cemetery—Memorial Park," *Cemetery Beautiful*, 1915, 14.

55 Kevin McNamara, "Cultural Anti-Modernism and 'The Modern Memorial-Park': Hubert Eaton and the Creation of Forest Lawn," *Canadian Review of American Studies* 32, no. 3, 2002.

57   Ibid.

57   *Time*, "The Happy Cemetery," August 24, 1942, http://www
.time.com/time/archive/preview/0,10987,849935,00.html?internalid
=related (August 19, 2004).

57   *Time*, "First Step Up to Heaven."

60   Ibid.

62–63   Ibid.

64   *Time*, "The Happy Cemetery."

65   Thomas Graves, "Keeping Ukraine Alive Through Death: Ukrainian-
American Gravestones as Cultural Markers," in Richard E. Meyer, ed.,
Ethnicity and the American Cemetery (Bowling Green, OH: Bowling
Green State University Popular Press, 1993), 51.

66   Kenneth T. Jackson and José Vergara Camilo, *Silent Cities: The Evolution of the American Cemetery* (New York: Princeton Architectural Press,
1989), 60.

66   John Matturi, "Windows in the Garden," in Richard E. Meyer, ed.,
Ethnicity and the American Cemetery (Bowling Green, OH: Bowling
Green State University Popular Press, 1993), 30.

69   Ibid., 23.

69   Ibid., 20.

74   "General Epitaphs," Everlife Memorials, 2000, http://www
.everlifememorials.com/headstones/epitaphs-general.htm (October 19,
2007).

75   Sloane, *The Last Great Necessity*, 230

76   Jo Ellen Davis, "Bob Waltrip Is Making Big Noises in a Quiet
Industry," *Business Week*, August 25, 1986, 66.

77–78   Robbie Byrd, "Her Last Wish: A 'Green' Burial," Huntsville Item, June
5, 2007, http://www.itemonline.com/archivesearch/local_story
_156005214.html (accessed October 15, 2007).

78   Steve Chawkins, "Nearer My Sod to Thee," *Los Angeles Times*,
December 10, 2003, A1+.

82 Hilary E. MacGregor, "Let Us Hit Pause and Reflect," *Los Angeles Times*, January 3, 2001, E1+.

82 Ibid.

84 Shaputis, "Funny Stories to Tickle Your Funny Bones."

84 Saving Graves, "El Dorado County," *Saving Graves*, March 25, 2003, http://www.usgennet.org/usa/ca/county/eldorado/ (October 17, 2007).

86 Brendan I. Koerner, "A Matter of Grave Import," *U.S. News and World Report*, June 12, 2000, 52.

89 Anonymous, *This Is a Cemetery*, n.d., http://www.ucalgary.ca/~dsucha/passage.html (October 18, 2007).

Barton, Bruce. "A Cemetery without Gloom." *Reader's Digest,* August 1937, 73–75.

Bathrick, Michael. "The 'Lulu' Carver of Richmond, MA." *BerkshireWeb*, N.d. http://www.berkshireweb.com/plexus/graveyards/rip.html (March 1, 2006).

Blaney, Herbert W. "Modern Park Cemetery." *American City*, April 1917, 395–401.

Brannon, Peter A. "Urn-Burial in Central Alabama," *American Antiquity* 3, no. 3 (January 1938): 228–235.

Carmack, Sharon DeBartolo. *Your Guide to Cemetery Research*. Cincinnati: Betterway Books, 2002.

Cedar Hilll Cemetery. "Jacob Weidenmann." *Cedar Hill Cemetery and Foundation*. 2005. http://www.cedarhillcemetery.org/Weidenmann.htm (March 20, 2007).

Chawkins, Steve. "Nearer My Sod to Thee." *Los Angeles Times*, December 10, 2003, A1+.

Chicora Foundation. *Grave Matters: The Preservation of African-American Cemeteries*. Columbia, SC: Chicora Foundation, 1996.

Chidester, David, and Edward T. Linenthal, eds. *American Sacred Space*. Bloomington: Indiana University Press, 1995.

Coffin, Margaret M. *Death in Early America*. New York: Elsevier / Nelson Books, 1976.

Colvin, Howard. *Architecture and the Afterlife*. New Haven, CT: Yale University Press, 1991.

Davis, Veronica A. *Here I Lay My Burdens Down: A History of Black Cemeteries of Richmond, Virginia*. Richmond: Dietz Press, 2003.

Deetz, James. *In Small Things Forgotten: An Archaeology of Early American Life.* New York: Anchor Books, 1996.

Etlin, Richard. *The Architecture of Death.* Cambridge, MA: MIT Press, 1984.

Farrell, James. *Inventing the American Way of Death 1830–1920.* Philadelphia: Temple University Press, 1980.

Fenn, Elizabeth A. "Honoring the Ancestors." *Southern Exposure,* September/October 1985, 42–47.

French, Stanley. "The Cemetery as Cultural Institution." Edited by David E. Stannard. *Death in America.* Philadelphia: University of Pennsylvania Press, 1975.

Gorn, Elliott J. "Black Spirits: The Ghostlore of Afro-American Slaves." *American Quarterly* 36, no. 4 (Autumn 1984): 549–565.

Jackson, Kenneth T., and José Vergara Camilo. *Silent Cities: The Evolution of the American Cemetery.* New York: Princeton Architectural Press, 1989.

Keister, Douglas. *Stories in Stone: A Field Guide to Cemetery Symbolism and Iconography.* Salt Lake City: Gibbs Smith Publisher, 2004.

Koerner, Brendan I. "A Matter of Grave Import." *U.S. News and World Report,* June 12, 2000, 52.

Kruger-Kahloula, Angelika. "On the Wrong Side of the Fence: Racial Segregation in American Cemeteries." In Geneviève Fabre and Robert G. O'Meally, eds. *History and Memory in African-American Culture.* New York: Oxford University Press, 1994.

Linden-Ward, Blanche. *Silent City on a Hill: Landscape of Memory and Boston's Mount Auburn Cemetery.* Columbus: Ohio State University Press, 1989.

MacGregor, Hilary E. "Let Us Hit Pause and Reflect." *Los Angeles Times,* January 3, 2001, E1+.

McNamara, Kevin. "Cultural Anti-Modernism and 'The Modern Memorial-Park': Hubert Eaton and the Creation of Forest Lawn." *Canadian Review of American Studies* 32, no. 3, 2002.

Meyer, Richard E., ed. *Ethnicity and the American Cemetery.* Bowling Green, OH: Bowling Green State University Popular Press, 1993.

Morris, Richard. *Sinners, Lovers, and Heroes: An Essay on Memorializing in Three American Cultures.* Albany, NY: SUNY Press, 1997.

New York Correction History Society. "City Cemetery, Hart Island (Potter's Field)." *City of New York Department of Corrections,* n.d. http://www.correctionhistory.org/html/chronicl/nycdoc/html/hart.html#Origin (October 17, 2007).

Pearson, Mike Parker. *The Archaeology of Death and Burial.* College Station: Texas A&M Press, 1999.

Pike, Martha V., and Janice Armstrong. "A Time to Mourn: Expressions of Grief in Nineteenth Century America." *Journal of Interdisciplinary History,* Vol. 13, No. 1 (Summer, 1982), pp. 151-152.

Rainville, Lynn. "African American Cemeteries in Albemarle and Amherst Counties." 2007. http://www.virginia.edu/woodson/projects/aacaac/index.shtml (October 17, 2007).

Shaputis, June. "Funny Stones to Tickle Your Funny Bones," *Webpanda.com,* 1998. http://www.webpanda.com/ponder/epitaphs.htm (February 20, 2004).

Sloane, David Charles. *The Last Great Necessity: Cemeteries in American History.* Baltimore, MD: Johns Hopkins University Press, 1991.

Stilgoe, John R. *Common Landscapes of America, 1580–1845.* New Haven, CT: Yale University Press, 1982.

Strangstad, Lynette. *A Graveyard Preservation Primer.* Nashville: American Association for State and Local History, 1988.

———. *Preservation of Historic Burial Grounds*. Information Series 76. Washington, DC: National Trust for Historic Preservation, 1993.

Time. "The Business of Dying," September 20, 1963. 2007. http://www.time.com/time/archive/preview/0,10987,870551,00.html (October 1, 2004).

———. "The Happy Cemetery." August 24, 1942. 2007. http://www.time.com/time/archive/preview/0,10987,849935,00.html?internalid=related (October 17, 2007).

Vo, Kim. "Cemeteries Increasingly Accommodate Different Cultures." *San Jose Mercury News*, April 13, 2004. http://www.mercurynews.com/mld/mercurynews/news/8383038.htm (June 15, 2004).

Weinel, Eleanor. "Ashes to Ashes, Dust to Dust: Is There Any Future for Cemeteries?" *USA Today Magazine*, January 1996, 48+.

Wright, Roberta Hughes, and Wilbur B. Hughes III. *Lay Down Body: Living History in African American Cemeteries*. Detroit: Visible Ink Press, 1996.

FURTHER READING AND WEBSITES

BOOKS

Colman, Penny. *Corpses, Coffins and Crypts: A History of Burials.* New York: Henry Holt and Company, 1997.

Perl, Lila. *Dying to Know.* New York: Twenty-First Century Books, 2001.

Ronan, Margaret, and Even Ronan. *Death around the World.* New York: Scholastic Book Services, 1978.

Sloan, Christopher. *Bury the Dead: Tombs, Corpses, Mummies, Skeletons & Rituals.* Washington, DC: National Geographic Books, 2002.

Turner, Ann Warren. *Houses for the Dead: Burial Customs through the Ages.* New York: David McKay Company, 1976.

Wilcox, Charlotte. *Mummies, Bones & Body Parts.* Minneapolis: Carolrhoda Books, 2001.

WEBSITES

African American Slave and Free Gravestones-Newport, Rhode Island
http://www.colonialcemetery.com
This website examines the relationship between slavery and Newport, Rhode Island, as well as discussing the African Americans who lived and died in this city.

Cemetery Preservation, Chicora Foundation
http://www.chicora.org/cemetery_preservation.htm
The website for the Chicora Foundation talks about its work saving and restoring old, forgotten cemeteries.

Farber Gravestone Collection
http://www.davidrumsey.com/farber/
This website contains images of the sculptures and stone carvings found on some of the United State's oldest gravestones.

GraveNet Project
http://edutel.musenet.org:8042/gravenet/index.html
This is an educational website, created to encourage students to study the
history, art, language, and symbols that can be found in local cemeteries.

Gravestone Glossary
http://www.primaryresearch.org/PRTHB/gravestones/index.php
This website provides a picture glossary of a multitude of images and symbols
found on gravestones.

History of African American Cemeteries
http://www.sciway.net/hist/chicora/gravematters-1.html
This website offers a detailed look at the history of African American burial
practices and cemeteries.

Mount Auburn Cemetery
http://www.mountauburn.org
This is the website for Mount Auburn Cemetery, a national landmark and the
first rural cemetery open to the public in the United States.

Pet's Rest: Cemetery, Crematory for Pet Animals
http://www.petsrest.com/
This website is the homepage for one of the most famous pet cemeteries in the
United States, Pet's Rest in Colma, California.

PHOTO ACKNOWLEDGMENTS